HE LOVES

Forever

Revised & Expanded Version

HE LOVES
Forever

The Enduring Message of God from the Old Testament

Thomas H. Olbricht

COLLEGE PRESS
PUBLISHING COMPANY
Joplin, Missouri

Table of Contents

To my Abilene Christian University students,

1967–

especially those serving the churches.

You sometimes taught me more than I taught you.

1
The Steadfast Love of God

*T*he story line of the Old Testament exudes love, excitement, and hope. It tells how this universe was made, and how humans, these inscrutable beings, occupied such a prominent position. It asserts that the Creator, before the creation of man and the universe, spoke into existence the vast reaches of space. Then he created man in his image. It tells of the Creator's love affair with creation and man. It affirms an undying, relentless, unceasing love, but not so much from the human side. Man not only is inexplicable, he is unstable, fickle, vacillating, and often faithless. But God is not man. As the Old Testament tells it, Israel's God loves — intensely — forever.

> O give thanks to the LORD, for he is good,
> for his steadfast love endures forever (Ps. 136:1).

The God of the Old Testament is an incessant lover.

I have not always thought of the Old Testament as captivating. I can understand people who say, "Well, I have read the Old Testament in parts, but I can't say I found it all that exciting. I too, in earlier years, tended to be turned off as I read in the Old Testament. Some of it I didn't understand, some of it seemed terribly outmoded, and long stretches, for example detailed rules for sacrificing, were downright boring." If you are among those who think the Old Testament is a vast wasteland, you are in good company. Among the detractors, you will find distinguished authors from this century as well as from times past.

I launched upon my first serious effort to read the Old Testament the summer I became a Christian at age sixteen. In the southern Missouri community in which I grew up, the sentiment prevailed that one should read the whole Bible before being baptized. I intended to complete my reading within a few months. Genesis went well. Parts were even exciting, such as when Joseph emerged as a powerful government official in Egypt. Exodus also moved. But after a couple of nights in Leviticus, I got bogged down, lost resolve and quit.

Months later, pricked by a bad conscience, I decided to "take the bull by the horns" and complete the task regardless of how slow the going. To get a running start, I went back to the opening book. Again, Genesis went well. In fact, it was even more exciting the second time around. And again I proceeded through Exodus with enough momentum to coast past the temple dimensions and the various metals in the vessels. Even the first part of Leviticus was a bit better. But about the middle of Leviticus, I ran out of gas. Part of the problem was that I couldn't make sense out of all the details. But most of all, I saw no relevance whatsoever for all those antiquated rules, and I wasn't familiar with anyone who really cared about them. Of course, I knew a few people who regularly read through the Bible, but they did it from a sense of duty. They didn't know what Leviticus meant either. It was several years later that I began to appreciate the Old Testament and even took up Leviticus in great anticipation.

The story line of the Old Testament is easier to follow if one is familiar with the basic contours. This book is designed to identify certain foundational affirmations in the Old Testament and to trace the threads which bind the whole together. We are concerned with the central message of the Old Testament.

Readers normally understand and appreciate the Old Testament only after a basic orientation. My wife and I made a trip to South America so we could teach missionaries. We had never been there before. We knew little about Brazil and Argentina (where we were to spend most of our time), and, before we went, we were around people who only had a passing interest in such regions. But we didn't want to arrive disoriented and uninformed. We bought three books on South America so as to learn its geography, people, culture, history, and intellectual outlooks. When we arrived, we faced some problems we weren't prepared for, but we were not disoriented because we had a basic feel for the situation. Through our prior consulting of these books, we were soon able to iron out unanticipated trouble spots.

In *He Loves Forever* we will basically scrutinize only one facet of Old Testament orientation — the central viewpoint. Scholars designate such a focus either the message of the Old Testament, Old Testament doctrine, or the theology of the Old Testament. Having been acclimated by this particular approach, one should then be able to make greater sense out of the writings in the Old Testament.

Love: The Foundation

Many artists have captured images of themselves in self-portraits. God sculpted a self-portrait in his Son for all to see. "No one has ever seen God. It is God the only Son, who is close to the Father's heart, who has made him known" (John 1:18). But even much earlier God painted a verbal picture of himself. In those awesome moments, as God conversed with Moses on the mountain, he declared for all to hear:

> "The LORD, the LORD, a God merciful and gracious, slow to anger, and abounding in steadfast love and faithfulness, keeping steadfast love for the thousandth generation, forgiving iniquity and transgression and sin, yet by no means clearing the guilty, but visiting the iniquity of the parents upon the children and the children's children, to the third and the fourth generation" (Exod. 34:6-7).

God's declaration links the two basic affirmations about him in the Old Testament. Notice the sequence, since the order is not accidental. First, God characterizes himself as a God of mercy, steadfast love, and faithfulness. But second — and some think this negates the first — God punishes the guilty. The order and emphasis of God's avowal runs counter to a typical man-in-the-mall's understanding of the Old Testament.

A conventional viewpoint, expressed with great conviction, is that the God of the Old Testament is a God of wrath, while the God of the New Testament is a God of love. A favorite example of God's wrath is the fire that came from the Lord to destroy Nadab and Abihu as they presided at the altar in the tabernacle (Lev. 10:1-3). A similar incident, however, is reported in the New Testament in respect to the deaths of Ananias and Sapphira, who supplied false information on the piece of property they had sold (Acts 5:1-11).

In contrast, the love of God is demonstrated in the New Testament, so it is observed with great confidence, through the parable of the prodigal son, which is placarded as the supreme affirmation of God's mercy and indefatigable love for wayward humankind. But the love of God is likewise vividly portrayed by Hosea in the Old Testament. Hosea depicted Israel as God's adopted son, raised by him from birth. Despite Israel's ingratitude and rebellion, God receives him back in mercy and forgiveness (Hos. 11:19). It is therefore unwise to declare that the wrath of God or the love of God is any more or less obvious in the Old Testament than in the New.

Despite popular opinion, the primary characteristic of God in the Old Testament is love. His love is intense and unremitting. His love is forever. This point cannot be stressed too much. The wrath of God is a secondary characteristic. The wrath of God neither supersedes love nor is independent from it. In fact, it is precisely because of God's intense love that his wrath pours forth on people who obstruct his efforts to achieve intimate communion with man.

Six Depictions of God

In Exodus 34:6-7, six terms are employed to depict God. We may subsume all these portrayals under the English word "love."

1. *Merciful*. The root of the Hebrew word translated mercy (*rhm*) means womb. It depicts the compassion of a mother for the child she has carried in her womb. God likewise exhibits an inner feeling of compassion or love for his human child which is expressed outwardly in helping action. He is a God whose divine love is manifested in his loving acts of compassion.

2. *Gracious*. The Hebrew root basically means to yearn towards, or long for. Here again, God is described as compassionate and merciful. He not only reacts toward humans as a mother toward her child, but he yearns for a close, intimate relationship.

3. *Slow to anger*. God's love is so momentous that his anger is long in coming. God's heart is always on his sleeve. His anger surfaces slowly and reluctantly.

4. *Steadfast love*. The Hebrew word *ḥsd* (*chesed*) is not simple to translate. The King James Version often translates *ḥsd*

"mercy," though on occasion "loving kindness." The New International Version simply uses "love," while the translators of the Revised Standard Version (as well as the New Revised Standard) prefer "steadfast love." The Revised Standard translation is instructive because it more fully captures the sense of the term. Perhaps the best text from which to understand *chesed* is Psalm 136. The line "for his steadfast love [*ḥsd*] endures forever" clearly shows that God's loving action on behalf of his people is inexhaustible. This term, more transparently than any other in the Old Testament, places in bold relief the central message. The God of Israel is simply a God who won't let up or give up. He is a God who loves forever, despite the rebellion and sinfulness of man.

5. *Faithfulness.* The Hebrew word employed here means "firmness" or "steadfastness." God is the one who is firm in resolve and action. He can be counted on. This trait of God is perhaps most clearly affirmed in Jeremiah.

> Thus says the LORD: If any of you could break my covenant with the day and my covenant with the night, so that day and night would not come at their appointed time, only then could my covenant with my servant David be broken . . . (Jer. 33:20-21).

God's love is never fickle. We can count on it just as we count on nightfall and daybreak.

6. *Forgiving.* The Hebrew word *nś'* (*nasa*) means "to lift up or remove." God is the one who, out of love, lifts up and pushes aside the sins of his people. On one hand, he removes the guilt of the wayward. On the other hand, in some cases he does not. There may be a problem here.

From these six descriptive terms, we learn first and foremost that God maintains a parent-like feeling for his children, and he is indefatigable in loving deeds of kindness on their behalf.

Man's Guilt and God's Love

Despite the fact that his fundamental characteristic is love, God "will by no means clear the guilty." What can we make of a loving God who still punishes those who defy his demands? We are now treading upon what I conceive as the profound center of the Old Testament understanding of the love of God. We will merely touch on it now, but later return to this concept more than once. It is clear that God won't "clear the guilty," because to do so would be to retreat from the intense love he has for creation. God loves his creation so much he desires continual, in-depth communion. He especially seeks an uninterrupted, highly personal relationship with man made in his image. The guilt of humankind is its incessant struggle to break free from the loving embrace of God. Humans are forever drawn toward alien relationships which obstruct companionship with God. Perhaps a person feels stifled, smothered, and suffocated by the intensity of God's concern and care. For whatever reason, she wanders off in an effort to escape the loving attention of God.

> All we like sheep have gone astray; we have all turned to our own way . . . (Isa. 53:6a).

But God is always in hot pursuit.

> Where can I go from your spirit? Or where can I flee from your presence? If I ascend to heaven, you are there; if I make my bed in Sheol, you are there. If I take the wings of the morning and settle at the farthest limits of the sea, even there your hand shall lead me, and your right hand shall hold me fast (Ps. 139:7-10).

God "will by no means clear the guilty" precisely because the guilty break the divine relationship. To live life by demands other than God's obstructs the personal relationship that God desires with each of his children. Therefore, he simply cannot "clear the guilty." To do so would be to give up on his commitment that his world be in intimate relationship with himself.

Understanding God's Plight

We might understand the plight of God by comparing his situation with that of a husband who has an unfaithful wife. (I certainly am not the first to use this analogy. It is used many times in the Old Testament, a stellar example being Hosea. Here we will merely modernize an ancient comparison.)

John meets Mary at a party. After a whirlwind courtship, they marry in a picturesque rock garden on a rare June day. John works for Monroe Business Machines and travels during the week. One night as she returns from the supermarket, Mary meets David in the parking lot of the apartment complex. In a few weeks they strike up a friendship. About a month later John comes home from a business trip. The dishes are stacked high, the bed is unmade, and the apartment is in general disarray. Mary is nowhere to be found. Sometime later she arrives home and explains she has been with David.

Now John could simply pass off the incident as an example of the liberation of modern woman. If he seemed indifferent to the whole matter, we would be justified in presuming that he didn't really love Mary after all. But if he introduced some sanction against her, such as saying, "Mary, I want you around when I get home, and if you aren't here next time, I will go out for dinner and not come home until midnight," we would assume that he really cared for Mary and wanted her home when he returned. If he simply "cleared the guilty" or rationalized her behavior with no sanction whatsoever, he would indicate that the relationship mattered little to him one way or the other. Likewise, God shows by his wrath that his love for wayward humanity is undying and deep. His sanctions against humans are the result of his incessant desire to bring man back into his fellowship (Amos 4:6-12).

God's intense love is the ground and explanation of his characteristics. In a real sense, this rousing declaration is central to the theology of the Old Testament:

> The steadfast love of the LORD never ceases, his mercies never come to an end; they are new every morning; great is your faithfulness (Lam. 3:22-23).

The circumstances under which the Lamentations' declaration is made makes it even more decisive. These words were uttered after the fall of Jerusalem in 587 B.C. Under the leadership of that powerful Babylonian emperor, Nebuchadnezzar, Jerusalem was completely destroyed. The walls were pushed over, and everything combustible was put to the torch. In the long siege prior to ultimate defeat, young children starved in the streets (Lam. 2:12), and apparently mothers even ate their own offspring so excruciating was their hunger (2:20). The conditions were unmistakably harrowing, and the author minced no words in expressing his bitterness (Lam. 3:1-21). He concluded the lament:

> He has made my teeth grind on gravel, and made me cower in ashes; my soul is bereft of peace; I have forgotten what happiness is; so I say, "Gone is my glory, and all that I had hoped for from the LORD" (Lam. 3:16-18).

But despite these disillusioning events, the author lifts up his heart in hope, "But this I call to mind, and therefore I have hope: The steadfast love of the LORD never ceases, his mercies never come to an end" (Lam. 3:21-22). Every characteristic of God must be appraised from the perspective of his love, which includes even his holiness, his righteousness, and his acting for the sake of his name.

Mighty Loving Actions

The love of God is obvious, not because of some misty sheen that hangs over his universe or an ecstatic emotion that overpowers the human heart, but because of his concrete, dramatic acts of salvation on behalf of his people.

The psalmist in Psalm 136:1 makes it obvious as to how he locates the steadfast love (*hsd*) of God. "O give thanks to the LORD, for he is good, for his steadfast love endures forever." He then goes on to pinpoint God's love in his action. First, God created the physical universe, the earth and the luminaries (Ps. 136:4-9). Second, he provided great victories for his people in Egypt and at the sea, and as they marched to the promised land and conquered it (136:10-22). These loving acts of God, though more dramatic in this past catalog of events, nevertheless continue. His salvific action endures forever (Ps. 136:23-25).

Since we are seeking the exciting story line of the Old Testament, it is imperative that we trace out these mighty acts of God. Psalms 105–106 and Nehemiah 9 clearly focus on those events. The mighty acts of God are obvious in his creation, in his concern for the fathers and, through them, the nations; in his bringing of his people out of Egypt; in his supporting and sustaining them in the wilderness; in his giving them the covenant and law through which he makes available goodness or blessings on a permanent basis; in his evicting the inhabitants of the land and turning it over to these landless peoples, that is, Israel; in the promise he makes to David. As we bring this book to a close we detail especially his reiteration of these actions and concerns through the Psalms, wisdom literature, and the elaborate depiction of new victories in apocalyptic materials. In each of these actions, the intensive, unremitting love of God for man is obvious.

Through the years I have asked students to set out their perspectives on the story line of the Old Testament. I have been impressed with how many begin with humans, not God. They focus on humankind as sinner; as constantly under the judgment of God. Or they may depict humans as always struggling, and often losing the battle in an effort to keep the commandments of the Maker. Of course, it is true that much time is spent in the Old Testament on wayward man. But it is unthinkable to begin the story line by focusing upon humankind. The first line of the Old Testament reads, "In the beginning when God created the heavens and the earth . . ." (Gen. 1:1). The last line reads, "Lo, I will send you the prophet Elijah before the great and terrible day of the LORD comes. He will turn the hearts of parents to their children and the hearts of children to their parents, so that I will not come and strike the land with a curse" (Mal. 4:5-6).

The Old Testament begins and ends with God, but, of course, as he relates to the universe and to humankind.

Questions for Discussion

1. On whom or what does the Old Testament focus?

2. What can aid one in setting out into the unexplored territory of the Old Testament?

3. What is the primary characteristic of God in the Old Testament?

4. Is the Old Testament God a God of wrath and the New Testament God a God of love?

5. Can wrath result from love?

6. It has been said that the opposite of love is indifference, not wrath. Wrath rather is a component part of love. Do you agree?

7. How does God characterize himself in Exodus 34:6,7?

8. Is God constantly giving up on humans over their perversity?

9. What is the context in which Lamentations 3:22,23 is written?

10. Is love the fundamental attribute of God?

11. Is God a fatherlike deity in the Old Testament?

12. Is it appropriate to argue that God is the focus of the Old Testament?

2
Goodness in Creation

*T*he first work of God was the creation of the physical universe. He himself preceded its existence and spoke it into being by the power of his word.

Lord, you have been our dwelling place in all generations. Before the mountains were brought forth, or ever you had formed the earth and the world, from everlasting to everlasting you are God (Ps. 90:1-2).

A perennial question is, why is there a world rather than none at all? The answer of Old Testament writers is that the world is here because God made it. The chief concern of Genesis, however, was not so much that God made the world, but his purpose in so doing. Genesis 1 tells us that God's motive for creating resides in his goodwill; his caring attitude toward what he has created. God said, "Let there be light." And when it appeared, "God saw that the light was good" (Gen. 1:4).

How does God's proclamation that light is good show his loving concern? Light serves a practical, useful purpose in the created order. And at the apex of the created order is man. The goodness of creation is that its various features and functions are mutually beneficial for man and the rest of creation. That creation is good therefore, in this case, is not a reflection upon its moral or aesthetic qualities. The declaration of the "goodness" of creation is expanded in Genesis 1:29-30: the plants and trees provide food for both man and beast. God contemplated how the features of creation complemented each other, and the writer of Genesis concludes, "God saw everything that he had made, and indeed, it was very good" (Gen. 1:31). God himself is good ("O give thanks to the Lord, for he is good"), and the created order he has produced is good, because his work in creation and history demonstrates that "his steadfast love endures forever" (Ps. 136:1).

Creation as Praise

The Old Testament reflects on the physical universe in a much different manner than twentieth century natural scientists do. Today's students of the universe see it as impersonal, unfeeling, inanimate, cold, material, and deterministic. From an Old Testament perspective, the universe itself is not to be unduly admired or worshiped, but rather its creator is to be praised for his loving kindness in making the universe functional and beneficial.

Of course, Genesis also knows another side of the universe, a deteriorated side that stands over against man as his enemy. By willfully turning their back on God, humans polluted and corrupted the earth and made it less than God intended. But the Old Testament writers cannot conceive of the universe merely through observing its overt characteristics. A scientist who envisions material reality without ethical dimensions may reflect on the destructive and aggressive features of the universe and declare that the universe is indifferent to the organisms found in it.

The Old Testament writers in contrast, commence with the conviction that a loving God works in and pervades the natural universe. They therefore cannot conceive of any feature of the universe as a study apart from God. It is likely that the earliest written comments on creation in Genesis were recorded after the exodus experience of delivery at the Sea. The Israelites stood in utter dismay with their backs to the sea and the Egyptians charging hard upon them. Suddenly and miraculously the sea opened up, and Yahweh (the Hebrew's special name for God) rescued his people. Because of this deed, he was obviously a God of love. The steadfast love of God, which Israel experienced, cast a whole new hue over her perception of the physical world.

Love has a way of making a qualitative difference. A story I often tell makes this point.

At the opening of the college year Steve sat by a girl in chapel.

"Hi. What's your name?"

"I'm Sue. Who are you?"

"Steve. Say-y-y Sue, where are you from?"

"Lueders. You probably never heard of it."

"No. Where is it?"

"Oh, it's about thirty miles north of Abilene."

"Small town, huh?"

"Yeah, about 600 people."

"I bet it's a real 'goat roper' place. They probably roll up the sidewalks by eight. Luederss-s. That's ludicrous!"

Steve continues to sit by Sue in chapel. One day he asks her for a date, then another and another. Finally, zap! It hits him! Now Lueders impresses Steve in an entirely different way. It is no longer Hicksville, but a quaint, rustic country village. The moon now shines romantically through the mesquite on the banks of the Clear Fork of the Brazos.

What was once contemptuous and ignoble is now warm and glowing.

With a mighty hand, God opened a path through the sea. The harshness of the earth was never again the same. The one who spoke to the sea is also the one who earlier spoke to the waters, gathering them in one place so that dry land appeared.

> "I will sing to the LORD, for he has triumphed gloriously; horse and rider he has thrown into the sea. The LORD is my strength and my might, and he has become my salvation; this is my God, and I will praise him, my father's God, and I will exalt him" (Exod. 15:1-2).

Israel could not separate God as savior from God as creator. The experience at the sea cast a whole new perspective upon material creation. Our public school education induces us to see the universe through the eyes of twentieth-century scientists. But as recipients of the love of God, we are moved to praise God for his creation. God met us with unutterable love in a place called Golgotha. Because he met us there, his world is forever warm, friendly and loving.

The Role of Man in Creation

In Genesis 1 God creates in days. In the first three days, God prepared the physical world for occupation, then in three successive days he created the beings that are to occupy it. These are paired as set forth in the chart below:

Day 1: Structure and light	Day 4: The luminaries
Day 2: Sky and water	Day 5: Birds and sea creatures
Day 3: Land and plants	Day 6: Land creatures and humans

In this sense the report on creation is arranged according to a logically prior criterion.

The goodness of creation especially reflects upon humans since they are the apex of creation. Furthermore, among all the creatures, man, that is, male and female, alone mirrors the very being of God. "Then God said, 'Let us make humankind in our image, according to our likeness'" (Gen.

1:26). As the result of that image, man has been charged with a special assignment.

> Be fruitful and multiply, and fill the earth and subdue it; and have dominion over the fish of the sea and over the birds of the air and over every living thing that moves upon the earth (Gen. 1:28).

Just as God exercises dominion over all reality, so man is given charge of the sphere in which God has placed him. Man therefore has been assigned a privileged position. But he is to exercise his dominion responsibly under God, protecting the interests of all the creatures as well as his own. As a result of our public school training, we are accustomed to thinking of humans merely as the most highly developed and complex of the earthly mammals, with skills of thought and organization exceeding those of any other. But the Old Testament goes one step further and sees humans as the purpose around which creation revolves. This is so because of their unique relationship with God (Ps. 8:4-8). Despite the fact that man is dust (Ps. 103:14; Gen. 2:7), he is "little less than God." He is the crown and glory of creation.

The order in which the creation occurs in Genesis 1–2 reflects not only chronological order, but also order according to rank. Many people have scrutinized Genesis to determine what it contributes to an understanding of how the earth and its creatures came about. Modern scientific thinking conditions us to take up everything in chronological order. We automatically read the Genesis account of creation from a chronological perspective. Apparently, however, the chronology was not as important to the author as the rank. Man ends up as the apex of creation in either case. The real point of Genesis 1–2 is often missed because of questions put to the text by modern scientists. The author knew nothing of modern science and its interests. He was intent upon recognizing the goodness of God because, for him, man stands in the center of the stage of life.

Curtain Call Order

In Genesis 1–2:4a, the order moves from the lowest to highest or from the least important to the most important. It's like curtain calls when a play ends. The stagehands appear first, then the bit players from the cast. After these minor players have taken their bows, the supporting actors and actresses appear. Last of all, as the grand finale, the stars of the show enter triumphantly.

God's first creative act was to speak the heavens and the earth into existence (1:1). These physical phenomena were in a very primitive state without order or structure (1:2). God set out to establish order instead of disorder, structure instead of chaos. He performed this great feat in order to provide a comfortable home for the one later to appear. He challenged darkness by calling forth light (1:3), and he set boundaries for darkness (1:4). Next he harnessed the waters, separating them by a firmament (1:7). He also circumscribed the waters on earth (1:9) so that dry land appeared (1:10). Once God had separated land from the chaotic waters, he spoke vegetation into existence (1:11). Light then was further refined and structured by the creation of the luminaries — the sun, moon, and stars — which determined the seasons, days, and years (1:14-18). Now God was ready to signal forth creatures from the sea and air (1:20). On the sixth day the land mammals appeared. And last of all, as the grand finale, God created man and gave him dominion over the rest of creation. The reason for the order of God's creating is therefore clear. God began at the most primitive level, then created higher and higher forms of existence until he came to man, the apex of creation. The early parts of creation constituted support systems for humankind.

Commencement Order

In Genesis 2:4b-25, the story of creation is retold with a new purpose. The interest shifts from the decisions of God in his heavenly council to the earth itself. Primal darkness, water, and the heavenly luminaries receive no attention. But the condition of earth receives immediate notice (2:4-6). After he created the earth and heavens, God formed man from the dust of the ground (2:7). This time the features of creation of less significance than man are mentioned last.

The order is again rank rather than chronology — as ranking in a commencement processional. The first person to march in the commencement line is the university president, followed by officers of the board, vice presidents, professors, associate professors, assistant professors, instructors, graduate candidates, bachelors, and finally associates in arts. Should the order be chronological rather than according to position, considerable changes would be required. A few bachelor candidates might come before the president because they are older.

In Genesis 2 man stands at the apex of creation just as in Genesis 1, but the order is reversed. In Genesis 2 his status is obvious not only because he is mentioned first, but also because he is the only being in whom God breathes the breath of life (2:7). After creating man, God made a garden paradise as a dwelling place that man would administer and in which he would labor (2:8-15). But none of the creatures in the garden was a proper companion for man, so God created woman from bone and flesh taken from the side of man. Woman appeared after animals, but ranked before them because her very being came from man who ranked first. She walks along beside the male having been taken from his side. She is to be his helper, not his servant. If she had been created to be his slave or servant Hebrew words are available to depict such a role. The Hebrew word employed makes clear that her status is helper, that is, one who fully shares life with the male as an equal.

These two accounts make identical affirmations in distinctive ways. They declare that the goodness and steadfast love of the Lord are obvious in his work in creation. He has given the male and female a distinctive role and created a realm that meets their many needs. Humans are indeed the most blessed of beings when they live by the rules of God. Creation itself declares that God loves forever.

The Roof Came Crashing Down

Even the best-laid plans go awry. God created the physical universe so it would be a blessing to the creatures in it, especially humans. But they decided to do it their own way rather than God's. Both Adam and Eve ate the fruit that God clearly stated they were not permitted to eat. Their action was catastrophic not only for them, but also for the physical order. Their decision is like a clumsy ten-year-old who knows nothing about watches but tries to make his Christmas digital work by tinkering in it with a ten inch screwdriver. Man didn't know what made the universe tick. God knew. He planned and executed it all. Man decided he could distinguish right from wrong as well as God, but he botched up what God had intended as a blessing. He brought creation crashing down around him.

Uneasiness about the material universe is justified despite the fact that it is a gift from a loving God. By his willful and unrelenting demands, man has polluted, corrupted, and emasculated God's physical creation. So it was from the beginning. According to Genesis 3:14-19, man's sinfulness caused snakes (and other animals, Hos. 2:18) to turn against him. He brought physical pain to women in childbirth (along with other illnesses). He caused the eking out of a living for the male to be a struggle against thistles, weeds, droughts, and depressions. Because of man's decision to travel his own path rather than God's, the earth turned into a pale semblance of the goodness intended by God. But it is not that because of man's sin the world became impersonal, indifferent, and mechanical. The impersonal world is a creation of modern thinkers. Man, in his eagerness to do what felt good, turned a blessing into a curse. So creation is a mixed bag. It retains the loving attention of God. But, at the same time, it suffers the ravages of man's sin.

As a teenager, I thought of the physical world as alienated and estranged from God. Preachers emphasized the fallen state and undesirability of the world. The favorite church songs depreciated the world and longed for the more blessed existence beyond.

> This world is not my home, I'm just a-passing through.
> My treasures are laid up somewhere beyond the blue;
> The angels beckon me from heaven's open door,
> And I can't feel at home in this world anymore.[1]

> Living below in this old sinful world,
>   Hardly a comfort can afford;
> Striving alone to face temptations sore,
>   Where could I go but to the Lord?[2]

When sin enters the world, the world is no longer ideal. This is true, however, not because the material order is evil. Man has brought about the evil. He has obstructed the goodness of God. The rest of creation is faithful to God. "Even the stork in the heavens knows its times; and the turtledove, swallow, and crane observe the time of their coming; but my people do not know the ordinance of the LORD" (Jer. 8:7).

---

[1] Arrangement copyright © 1937 by Albert E. Brumley. Renewal copyright © 1965 by Albert E. Brumley & Sons, Powell, Missouri 65730. All rights reserved. Used by permission.

[2] Copyright © 1940 by Stamps-Baxter Music & Printing Co. Renewal copyright © 1968. All rights reserved. Used by permission.

Man gummed up the works. A loving God made the universe. It is not threatening, contaminated, or chaotic by nature. The universe endangers man's existence because of his distorted use of it. The one who trusts God, while realizing that nature has been tarnished, nevertheless recognizes in the material order the work of a loving creator.

The Open Hand of the Lord

The love of God is obvious also in the maintenance of the physical world. In the Old Testament the steadfast love of the Lord is evident in creation itself because of God's continuing work in it. The universe exists moment by moment because of God's abiding presence. His word, his look, and his work determine whether it is productive and fruitful. When his hand is opened, when he looks upon creation, and when his face shines upon the created order, all goes well. But when his hand closes and his face darkens and turns away, creation suffers. The famous "Prayer of Benediction" (Num. 6:24-26) recognizes that man's welfare depends upon God's continued work in the created order:

> The LORD bless you and keep you; the LORD make his face to shine upon you, and be gracious to you; the LORD lift up his countenance upon you, and give you peace.

God did not bring the physical universe into existence then rest forever after as the Deists would have it. He continues to give it existence. He is creator and sustainer.

Psalm 104 emphasizes God's sustaining relationship with creation. This psalmist obviously was not weighed down by how human sin reduced the goodness of the material order. He was convinced that through all the flaws and smudges the work of God was still obvious (Ps. 104:27-30).

We live in a time when people search for scientific answers to any question whatever about the physical universe. The reason, of course, is the amazing success of the scientific community in discovering the cause of smallpox, the air waves through which we receive television signals, basic features of the universe such as black holes and additional moons around Jupiter, minute particles such as quarks from which all matter is derived, and now especially, computer technology. But there are certain questions that no scientist in his right mind even pretends to answer on scientific grounds. The psalmist, however, boldly steps in where angels fear to tread. He supplies the answer to such questions.

The questions I have in mind are like this: Why are there trees rather than none at all? Now botanists, in fact, answer the question: How is it possible that there are trees? They explain that roots extract nutrients from the soil by molecular action. These nutrients are carried through the layers under bark to the leaves where photosynthesis occurs, building organic compounds from carbon dioxide and water. The basic scientific question is: How is that? The scientific community has provided many impressive answers to these questions. But to my first question (Why are there trees rather than none at all?), they have no answers. There are no apparent, inherent reasons why trees exist, though obviously they do contribute certain qualities which balance the ecological systems.

The psalmist was not really concerned with this sort of question. He does not tell us how trees grow. But he does tell us why they grow, a question which evades the expertise of botanists. There are trees because God created them for the benefit of the creatures that roam the earth.

> You cause the grass to grow for the cattle, and plants for people to use, to bring forth food from the earth, and wine to gladden the human heart, oil to make the face shine, and bread to strengthen the human heart. The trees of the LORD are watered abundantly, the cedars of Lebanon that he planted. In them the birds build their nests; the stork has its home in the fir trees (Ps. 104:14-17).

So a loving God created a world in which the basic features complement and assist one another. This world continues because God sustains it. The loving hand of God is even obvious in light and darkness. God made the moon to mark the seasons and the sun to provide daylight hours (104:19). Darkness is no absence or accident. God made the darkness (104:20) for a definite purpose. Light and darkness delineate the division of labor among earth's creatures. The lions prowl at night and obtain their food under the cover of darkness. Humans are assigned the daylight shift. The lion's shift ends, and humans get up and go to work. Lions and humans do not get in each other's way because daylight and darkness prescribe their respective work periods (Ps. 104:21-23).

Even the creatures of the sea have their assigned role, including the dreaded Leviathan (Ps. 104:26), whom God created as a plaything. (For more on the Leviathan, see Isa. 27:1.)

Lovely for Me

Most of us were taught when young to view creation as the loving work of God. God sends the rain. He makes the warm sunshine. He creates the beautiful flowers. He gives me my parents. He supplies my food. God loves me. My parents love me. The world is friendly and loving. But somehow we have lost that vision. Perhaps the conviction of the Old Testament writers can help us recover it. A popular child's song reflects the Old Testament approach to creation as praise. It might embarrass sophisticated adults, but it shouldn't.

> Climb up the mountain, point to the sun.
>   Notice the grasses, count every one.
> Measure the rainbow, sail o'er the sea.
>   God made the whole world lovely for me.
>
> Open your ears the birds sweetly sing.
>   Open your eyes to wonderful things.
> Look all around you, beauty you'll see.
>   God made the whole world lovely for me.[3]

So we reiterate:

> The steadfast love of the LORD never ceases, his mercies never come to an end; they are new every morning; great is your faithfulness. "The LORD is my portion," says my soul, "therefore I will hope in him" (Lam. 3:22-24).

---

[3] Source unknown.

Questions for Discussion

1. Why, according to the Old Testament, is there a universe rather than none at all?

2. What is meant by, "And God saw that it was good"?

3. How do contemporary scientists characterize the universe?

4. Why do Old Testament writers characterize it differently?

5. What are the implications of the Old Testament claim that God is both creator and savior?

6. What is the rationale behind what God created in each of the six days?

7. Why are humans created last in Genesis 1?

8. Is the woman created by God to be subservient to the male?

9. What caused the earth to be less desirable than what God intended?

10. Does the Old Testament support the right of humans to do whatever they wish with their physical environment?

11. Did God cease to work in the universe after the close of the Scriptures?

12. Can scientists tell us why there are trees rather than none at all?

3
Blessings through Abraham

The author of Genesis believed that God is loving and good and that he created the universe and man because of his desire to share his blessings. He declared that God set out to share his love and gifts with everyone. Even from the first, God was no respecter of persons. He had no favorites among his children. He treated everyone alike in terms of his desire to bless. He did, however, call Israel to be a special people. It was not, however, so as to shower all his gifts on Israel alone and place them on a pedestal. He called them to be servants to the nations; to be the conduit through whom his gifts would be distributed.

But didn't God, in fact, show favoritism to Israel? Jews and Christians down through the centuries have assumed he did. Why did God go out of his way to tap Abraham on the shoulder? "Then I took your father Abraham from beyond the River and led him through all the land of Canaan and made his offspring many" (Josh. 24:3). Why did he specially bless Jacob (Gen. 30:30)? Why did he take land from the Amorites and the king of Bashan and give it as a "heritage to

Israel" (Ps. 136:22)? Surely God exhibited favoritism in these instances. Why did God make special promises to the fathers, and through them to the nation Israel? "I will bring you into the land that I swore to give to Abraham, Isaac, and Jacob; I will give it to you for a possession. I am the LORD" (Exod. 6:8). The answer to these questions — because he loves everyone — is the focus of this chapter.

The Promise

The promise of God to Abraham is the central declaration in the book of Genesis, if not in the whole Old Testament.

> Now the LORD said to Abram: "Go from your country and your kindred and your father's house to the land that I will show you. I will make of you a great nation, and I will bless you, and make your name great, so that you will be a blessing. I will bless those who bless you, and the one who curses you I will curse; and in you all the families of the earth shall be blessed" (Gen. 12:1-3).

Notice three items in this promise. First, God singled out one man, Abram, for a special assignment. Second, he did this to bless Abram and his seed. Third, this action of God did not constitute favoritism to Abram and his descendants. God singled out Abram so that "all the families of the earth shall be blessed." Abram was selected (or elected) not just to elevate him to VIP status. Rather, he was singled out for a special assignment. He was to be God's blessed man, so that the nations would also be blessed. He was like a warehouse receiving the good gifts of God. In turn, he was to open the doors of that warehouse so all the peoples of the multifold nations could enter and claim God's magnificent gifts. He was called to be God's special servant. In the same manner, the descendants of Abraham received the identical assignment (Ps. 136:21-22; Isa. 49:6).

Through this promise God declared his intent to love everyone — all peoples and nations.

Events Leading to the Promise

To discover the reason and context for God's promise to Abraham, we need to backtrack to the beginning. Immediately before the promise, the confusion of language disrupted life (Gen. 11). Men could no longer understand each other. So not only were humans estranged from God, they also were estranged from one another. As the story unfolds in Genesis, it is obvious that the promise is God's means of renewing his blessings to all humankind after they had been cut off by sin.

God lovingly created the heavens and earth, then plants and animals, and finally man. The earth was good and a blessing, especially for man made in God's image. God gave humans the rules for enjoying creation. But the woman and man were tempted, and they decided to go their own way and make their own rules. The result was much like a locomotive deciding to wander off the tracks to visit the gushing springs and woodland flowers. Locomotives aren't made for running except upon tracks. The outcome for man was a similar disaster because he was created to run on tracks laid by God.

Humans were evicted from the garden and brought down upon themselves problems and disasters. Things went from bad to worse. Cain killed Abel (Gen. 4:8) and became a fugitive (4:12). Humans lusted more and more (Gen. 6:1-4) and threw restraints to the wind. Finally, man turned so far from God that "every intent of the thoughts of his heart was only evil continually" (Gen. 6:5).

At that point, God looked upon the human situation as almost hopeless. He created man for fellowship with himself, but man ignored divine fellowship and set out on his own to pollute and contaminate creation. So God decided to rid the earth of the scourge (man) with a gigantic flood. Because of one righteous man (Noah), a remnant was preserved for a new start. God's action should have taught man a lesson, but soon he was back to his old tricks having it his way rather than God's. The youngest son of Noah observed his father's nakedness and was cursed. Later descendants determined to show God a thing or two and proceeded to build a tower reaching into the heavens so they could make a name for themselves. They hadn't learned the lesson at all. God had no choice but to disrupt their life, hoping that they would come to their senses and return to him.

After all these miscues, the situation seemed hopeless, but God had a plan. He still wished to bless all men and through them bless creation itself. How could he do it? The text tells us his plan entailed the calling of a man. Through that man and his descendants the nations would be blessed. How was God to bless everyone through one man and his family? Genesis and the rest of the Old Testament clearly provide the answer to that question. But why did God decide to do it this way? For example, why didn't God simply speak as he did later in the wilderness and supply man with all his needs? He supplied the heavenly bread, manna, and the quail on the winds from the south, and water from the rock. If God wants to bless creation, why doesn't he shower on it every want and whim for which man can dream? We do not have a clear answer from the text, but there are hints, especially in the affirmation that God acts for the sake of his name (see chapter five).

Simply passing out gifts often hinders rather than helps. It is common to walk down the street in an inner city and be accosted by a homeless person soliciting a dollar for a meal. Anyone knows by sizing up the situation that the money will not go for a meal but for alcohol. Answering the request will not really help, but only compound a syndrome leading the person to disaster. The person at risk really needs to get back on the right track of life so that the money can really contribute to his welfare. In the same manner when God distributes his gifts, he seeks out ways to point men in the right direction so they can genuinely utilize his good gifts.

Fulfilling of the Promise

Through these specially selected servants God renewed the sharing of his love and goodness with man and the universe. He will bless Abraham and his descendants and in turn bless those with whom they rub shoulders. We have accented the promise made to Abraham. The same promise is repeated to Isaac (Gen. 26:4) and Jacob (Gen. 28:13-14). God promises to form a "great nation" through whom the promise will be kept alive and fulfilled. It is an open-ended promise. Paul says Christ fulfilled the promise (Gal. 3:16). Christ is the ultimate fulfillment, but it is wrong to conclude that God did nothing to bless the nations between Abraham and Christ. Genesis makes it perfectly clear that even from the time he first spoke to Abraham, God was blessing the peoples through these chosen servants. Wherever God's man or woman is located, there God's good gifts are being distributed.

The Blessing through Abraham

Abraham was blessed by God. "Now Abram was very rich in livestock, in silver, and in gold" (Gen. 13:2). And his wealth rubbed off on those around him. Abraham had two brothers, Nahor and Haran. Haran died young and left a son named Lot (Gen. 11:27,28,31). When Abraham traveled west, Lot went along. Because of his relationship with Abraham, he too became very wealthy, so wealthy that Abraham and Lot had to separate their herds and flocks. No one region could supply adequate pasture (Gen. 13:6). Lot liked the Jordan Valley, and he took his family in that direction to live in Sodom. That move soon created problems since "the people of Sodom were wicked, great sinners against the LORD" (Gen. 13:13). But when a coalition of five kings attacked these towns, Abraham came to the rescue. He declined booty for his exploits because God had called him to bless others (Gen. 14:21-24). The wickedness of Sodom later became so great that God determined to destroy the city (Gen. 18:17). Despite the city's sinfulness, however, destruction was delayed because of the promise to Abraham (Gen. 18:18) and Lot's relationship with him. Where Abraham and his descendants are found, there the blessings of God surface. From the loins of Lot came two nations, Moab and Ammon (Gen. 19:37-38). These nations were also blessed because of their relationship with Israel (Deut. 2:9,19).

In a few instances, however, Abraham brought a curse on the nations — such as Egypt (Gen. 12) and Philistia (Gen. 20) — because of his deceit. But in these stories, we discover that when the deception was uncovered and a wrong relationship was righted, blessings followed the curse. "Then Abraham prayed to God: and God healed Abimelech, and also healed-his wife and female slaves so that they bore children. For the LORD had closed fast all the wombs of the house of Abimelech because of Sarah, Abraham's wife" (Gen. 20:17-18).

The Blessing through Isaac

Isaac himself later traveled to Philistia during a drought. The Lord appeared in Gerar and repeated the promise, "And I will make your offspring as numerous as the stars of heaven; and will give to your offspring all these lands; and all the nations of the earth shall gain blessings for themselves through your offspring" (Gen. 26:4). Just as Abraham became wealthy, so Isaac grew in affluence in Philistia. "Isaac sowed seed in that land, and in the same year reaped a hundredfold. The LORD blessed him, and the man became rich; he prospered more and more until he became very wealthy;" (Gen. 26:12-13). After a time the Philistines "envied him," and apparently thought he was becoming wealthy at their expense (Gen. 26:14). So they harassed him along with his flocks and

herds and requested that he leave the country (26:16). It did-
n't occur to the Philistines that not only was Isaac being
blessed, but they were also prospering because of Isaac's presence. His affluence, in fact, was not at their expense. Because
Isaac and his people were in the land, the Philistines were
instead being blessed.

After a time, Abimelech sized up the situation and saw
things as they really were. He realized that Isaac's wealth was
the result of God's action. So Abimelech took some of his
important men and went to talk with Isaac. He said, "We see
plainly that the LORD has been with you . . . . You are now
the blessed of the LORD" (Gen. 26:28-29). Abimelech had
concluded that if he were to enter into a covenant with Isaac,
he too would be blessed and not cursed. Isaac was God's man.
And wherever there is a man of God, good things are hap-
pening. A community is blessed by the presence of God's
woman or God's man.

A family of Christians lived in a community. Whenever
anyone was sick, the wife baked a pie and took it over. If the
ill person was in the hospital, they paid a visit. If a neighbor
needed to borrow tools, to get advice, or to ask for assistance,
the family always gave it willingly and freely. At holiday times
they often invited neighbors over for a get-together. The reaction in the community was mixed. Everyone thought they
were good people; everything seemed to go their way. Their
children did very well in school. After they graduated from a
religious college, they were able to get very good jobs. After
some years, the company the man worked for transferred him
out of state. It was only then that the neighbors recognized
how blessed they had been. The people who replaced them
spent their extra hours attending and giving cocktail parties.
They didn't notice what was going on in the neighborhood. If
anyone became ill or needed help, they were oblivious to it
all. Their children were undisciplined. They were destructive
to trees in the park, they damaged other people's property,

and were cruel to animals. In general, they were "a pain in the neck."

After six months of the new neighbors, the community woke up and realized that, though they had secretly envied the family committed to God, they had indeed been blessed beyond measure by their presence. We need to realize that as God's people, wherever we are, we are a storehouse from which the gifts of God are being distributed. "I will bless you, and through you will the nations be blessed." The servant of God may be envied and ridiculed, like Isaac was. But he has no reason for a low self-image. Through her or him the community is being blessed whether it recognizes it or not.

The Blessing through Jacob

Jacob was a conniver. Perhaps he got it from his mother's side of the family since both Rebekah and Laban conspired to get ahead. Through a ruse involving both Rebekah and Jacob, Jacob received the blessing from Isaac that was intended for Esau (Gen. 27:5-29). Even though human deceit led to the reversed blessing, the text implies that the hand of God was involved all along. At the birth of the twins, the Lord told Rebekah that "the elder shall serve the younger" (Gen. 25:23). And according to Malachi at the end of the Old Testament, God said, "I have loved Jacob but I have hated Esau" (Mal. 1:2-3). Is this story an example for us? Does the action of Rebekah represent the morals of a different age and time? No! In fact, such duplicity was likely even more shocking then than now, especially since Isaac was blind and old. Such persons were to be revered and helped, not duped (Deut. 28:18; Lev. 19:32).

So what point is God trying to make through this text? The point for Israel apparently is that Jacob received his heritage as a gift, not by natural or legal rights. The people of Israel received their land for the same reason. And a Christian attains his or her status the same way. All of this shows that God moves in mysterious ways his wonders to perform.

Jacob spent much of his life trying to get ahead by tricking his relatives and associates. He had the heart of a conniver. He for many years attributed his good fortune to his own craftiness. In later times, however, as he reflected on his successes, he concluded that it may not have been his machinations after all, but rather the blessings that God intended and brought about.

> If the God of my father, the God of Abraham and the Fear of Isaac, had not been on my side, surely now you would have sent me away empty-handed. God saw my affliction and the labor of my hands, and rebuked you last night (Gen. 31:42).

It may well be the case that even we, when we survey our life and congratulate ourselves on our accomplishments, must also confess that in the final analysis, we too seem to have received assistance from beyond. We too detect forces at work unaccounted for when we truthfully assess our own abilities.

Esau was exceedingly angry about the whole matter, as we might expect. Life at home became uncomfortable. Furthermore, Rebekah decided she wanted Jacob to take a wife from her own people, so she arranged for Jacob's departure (Gen. 27:41-46). So Jacob left Palestine for Haran, the home of Rebekah's family. On the way he stopped one night, put a stone under his head, and fell asleep. He dreamed about angels ascending and descending on a ladder reaching to the sky (Gen. 28:10-13). At the top of the ladder was the Lord, and he repeated the promise to Jacob which he had made to his grandfather Abraham and his father Isaac: "And your offspring shall be like the dust of the earth and you shall spread abroad to the west and the east and to the north and the south; and all the families of the earth shall be blessed in you and in your offspring" (Gen. 28: 14).

Jacob finally arrived in Haran and stopped at a well where the shepherds watered their flocks. At the well he met Rachel, the daughter of Laban, Rebekah's brother. She took him to meet the family, and he fell in love with her. When Laban asked Jacob what his wages would be for working for him, Jacob was ready with an answer. He would take Rachel as a wife. So Jacob worked for seven years and the wedding day was set (Gen. 29:20). But Laban had concocted a way to get seven more years from Jacob. He slipped Leah in the wedding tent in the place of Rachel. So Jacob had to put in seven more years for Rachel. When the second seven were up, Jacob requested permission to return home. During all those years Laban had done very well. He wanted to know the source of his prosperity, and, through some sort of divination, Laban found out that "the LORD has blessed me because of you" (Gen. 30:27). Jacob agreed. "For you had little before I came, and it has increased abundantly; and the LORD has blessed you wherever I turned" (Gen. 30:30). And not only was Laban blessed, but when Jacob left, having introduced a few stratagems of his own, Jacob had grown "exceedingly rich, and had large flocks, and male and female slaves, and camels and donkeys" (Gen. 30:43).

The Blessing to All the Nations through Joseph

Many nations were blessed because of the presence of God's people — and because they were related to Abraham. These included the Canaanites, Egyptians, Philistines, Ishmaelites, Ammonites, Moabites, Edomites, and, through Jacob, the Arameans. But with Joseph all the nations were blessed. His presence as a man of God in Egypt not only brought a blessing on Egypt, but also the nations.

Joseph got to Egypt in the first place because his brothers were jealous that he was Jacob's favorite son. Furthermore, he went around reporting on dreams which declared that his brothers would be his servants. So the brothers sold

Joseph to traveling slave traders, and he was taken to Egypt. Joseph was God's man and wherever he went, the blessing of the Lord followed.

In Egypt Joseph was bought by Potiphar, a captain in Pharaoh's guard (Gen. 39:1). Because he was God's man, things went well. "His master saw that the LORD was with him, and that the LORD caused all he did to prosper in his hand" (Gen. 39:3). The language of Genesis 39:5 makes it certain that the author had in mind the promise to Abraham, Isaac, and Jacob:

> From the time that he made him overseer in his house and over all that he had, the LORD blessed the Egyptian's house for Joseph's sake; the blessing of the LORD was on all that he had, in house and field.

Joseph's stay in Potiphar's house did not last. Because of the illicit desires of Pharaoh's wife, Joseph ended up wasting away in prison. But even in prison Joseph was God's person, and those who rubbed shoulders with him even there were blessed. The imprisoned butler of Pharaoh received from Joseph a favorable interpretation of a dream and was returned to favor. But Joseph remained in prison two more years even though the butler promised he would remember him (Gen. 40:23–41:1). At that time, Pharaoh had a dream and no one could interpret it. Finally, the butler remembered Joseph, and Pharaoh had Joseph brought in to tell him what the dream meant. Joseph explained that seven excellent crop years would be followed by seven years of drought, so Pharaoh assigned Joseph the task of storing up grain for the years of famine. When the seven good years were past, enough grain had been stored to carry the Egyptians through the famine. They also had enough grain for other countries. People came from everywhere seeking food. So with Joseph in Egypt it actually occurred that, through a seed of Abraham, all the nations were blessed. The author must have remembered the promise to Abraham, repeated to Isaac and Jacob as he told of individuals from the various nations arriving in Egypt to buy grain.

> And since the famine had spread over all the land, Joseph opened all the storehouses, and sold to the Egyptians, for the famine was severe in the land of Egypt. Moreover, all the world came to Joseph in Egypt to buy grain, because the famine became severe throughout the world (Gen. 41:56-57).

This distribution of the good gifts of the earth became a paradigm out of which Israel understood her function on earth. Israel has been assigned by Yahweh to superintend the warehouse from which the good gifts of God are distributed to the whole earth.

No doubt there were periods along the way when Joseph wondered how anything of significance could result from his life. He went from bad to worse, from his father's house to slavery, to prison. But finally a turnaround occurred, and when it did, he ended up controlling the food supplies for the whole earth. Joseph could see the involvement of the Lord (Gen. 50:20-21).

The Lord had in mind all the time that Joseph would be his servant through whom he would bless the nations. So we too, not knowing the outcome of our life's work, proceed by faith, knowing that when our life is over we can discern how God has worked through us to bless the peoples who inhabit this globe.

A Light to the Nations

The prophets clearly envisioned Israel as a servant to the nations.

> He says, "It is too light a thing that you should be my servant to raise up the tribes of Jacob and to restore the survivors of Israel; I will give you as a light to the nations, that my salvation may reach to the end of the earth" (Isa. 49:6).

> Many nations shall come and say, "Come, let us go up to the mountain of the LORD, to the house of the God of Jacob; that he may teach us his ways and that we may walk in his paths." For out of Zion shall go forth his instruction, and the word of the LORD from Jerusalem (Micah 4:2).

> Thus says the Lord GOD: On the day that I cleanse you from all your iniquities, I will cause the towns to be inhabited, and the waste places shall be rebuilt. The land that was desolate shall be tilled, instead of being the desolation that it was in the sight of all who passed by. And they will say, "This land that was desolate has become like the garden of Eden; and the waste and desolate and ruined towns are now inhabited and fortified." Then the nations that are left all around you shall know that I, the LORD, have rebuilt the ruined places, and replanted that which was desolate; I, the LORD, have spoken, and I will do it (Ezek. 36:33-36).

In the promise to the fathers, God made known his plan for distributing his good gifts. From the beginning humans turned their back on the God-given guidelines and contaminated the good order God established. God, however, never gives up. Because of Yahweh's persistence, his love is always a viable and living option. God's people are special to him. But his intent is not simply to elevate them above their fellows, and supply their every wish and whim. He has designated them the supply house through whom the nations are blessed.

> He is mindful of his covenant forever, of the word that he commanded, for a thousand generations, the covenant that he made with Abraham, his sworn promise to Isaac, which he confirmed to Jacob as a statute, to Israel as an everlasting covenant (Ps. 105:8-10).

Questions for Discussion

1. Did Yahweh have eyes for Israel alone?

2. Why did God bless Abraham and his descendants?

3. Does the blessing of the nations await the death of Christ?

4. How did Abraham bless other nations?

5. What nation did Isaac bless?

6. Why was the blessing through Jacob rather than Esau?

7. Did the conniving of Jacob clearly advance his own interests?

8. How did Joseph bless all the nations?

9. What role did Isaiah assign to the people of Israel?

10. Is Yahweh's chief purpose to look out for his own people?

11. Where are the nations located that were blessed by the patriarchs?

12. Does God assign Christians the task of overseeing his warehouse?

4
Deliverance in the Exodus

After a long time the king of Egypt died. The Israelites groaned under their slavery, and cried out. Out of their slavery their cry for help rose up to God. God heard their groaning, and God remembered his covenant with Abraham, Isaac, and Jacob (Exod. 2:23-24).

About 600 years after the promise of God to Abraham, his descendants groaned under slavery in Egypt. Six hundred years is a long time. It is longer than the period from when Columbus sailed to America or Martin Luther nailed his ninety-five theses to the church door until today. Less than 400 years ago the Pilgrims left England and landed at Plymouth Rock. Even after 600 years God remembered his promise to bless his people and through them the nations. God loves forever. God loves every person made in his image. God loves people in all kinds of circumstances. God even loves slaves. And he loves to free them from slavery.

But God's helping hand of love reaches out only when people cry out for help. The book of Judges makes this point clear. When the people were self-satisfied, thinking they had it made, God's help receded over the horizon. God stepped in only after they recognized they could not make it on their own and cried out to him (Judg. 3:9).

Strange as it may seem, it is possible to help only those who want to be helped. Often a child trying to get a dress on a doll has all kinds of trouble, and flares up with complaints. "Here, give me the doll," we say, and pull it away. We put the dress on, straighten it, and give the doll back. The child cries out, "I don't want it that way," and tugs at the garment, popping a button; then, after tearing the dress, throws it on the floor.

God knows that people who insist on living on their own terms cannot be helped. "Therefore God also gave them up in the lusts of their hearts to impurity, to the degrading of their bodies among themselves" (Rom. 1:24). God forever desires relationship with humans. He is more than ready to help people who seek him out, people who realize that all human solutions are temporary and inadequate, if not ruinous. The helping hand of God always comes to aid his people when they have their backs to the wall and genuinely seek his aid. God loves people who are down and out and enslaved. He is eager to release the captive and break their yoke of bondage.

The Importance of the Exodus

In parts of the Old Testament where the mighty acts of God are heralded and reiterated (Deut. 26:5-11, Ps. 105-106), three events stand out: (1) the promise of God to Abraham, Isaac, and Jacob, (2) the events in Egypt and at the sea, and (3) the conquest of the land. The second event takes a central role because the Passover, a commemoration of the Egyptian event, was the most important of the feasts in some periods of Old Testament history. For example, in the restoration of religion under Josiah, the historian emphasizes an extensive celebration of the Passover (2 Kgs. 23:21-23). Also, the prophets often depicted the ingratitude of the people by charging that they had forgotten the exodus.

> O my people, what have I done to you? In what have I wearied you? Answer me! For I brought you up from the land of Egypt, and redeemed you from the house of slavery; and I sent before you Moses, Aaron, and Miriam (Micah 6:3-4).

> When Israel was a child, I loved him, and out of Egypt I called my son. The more I called them, the more they went from me; they kept sacrificing to the Baals, and offering incense to idols (Hos. 11: 1-2).

Finally, Yahweh identified himself in the covenant:

> I am the LORD your God, who brought you out of the land of Egypt, out of the house of slavery (Exod. 20:2).

The period of the exodus is a crucial time. In that period God (1) revealed his new name, (2) created a new nation of faith in himself, and (3) made believers out of the nations.

I Am Yahweh

After the death of Joseph, the descendants of Jacob remained in Egypt four hundred years. As time passed, the Egyptians forgot they were being blessed because of the Israelites. Not only was Israel's presence a blessing, but Jacob himself blessed the Pharaoh. "Then Joseph brought in his father Jacob, and presented him before Pharaoh, and Jacob blessed Pharaoh" (Gen. 47:7). "Now a new king arose over Egypt, who did not know Joseph"(Exod. 1:8). This new king enslaved the people of God and became a curse to them rather than a blessing. "I will bless those who bless you, and the one who curses you I will curse; and in you all the families of the earth shall be blessed"(Gen. 12:3). But God prefers to bless, so he made plans to end the curse by calling a man, Moses, to lead his people out of Egypt to the land promised to Abraham many centuries earlier.

God appeared to Moses on a mountain in Midian. Attracted by a burning bush, Moses drew near to see the spectacle. God spoke out of the fire, revealed his plans, and told Moses he was sending him to Pharaoh. "So come, I will send you to Pharaoh to bring my people, the Israelites, out of Egypt" (Exod. 3:10). When God said this, Moses drew back in fear, probably not because he was afraid of the Pharaoh, but because he worried over the reception of the people when he told them the news. After all, some had already rejected his leadership (Exod. 2:14). Then Moses said to God, "If I come to the Israelites and say to them, 'The God of your ancestors has sent me to you,' and they ask me, 'What is his name?' what shall I say to them?" (Exod. 3:13). God replied, "I AM WHO I AM" (Exod. 3:14). This English phrase is a translation of the Hebrew verb *hayah,* which is equivalent to the infinitive "to be." The next verse affirms clearly that from this Hebrew root comes "Yahweh," translated consistently in the New Revised Standard Version as LORD. (For further information on the translation, see the middle section of the preface to the NRSV).

The standard Semitic word for God is *elohim.* It is often found in the Old Testament (e.g., Gen. 1:1). The way Moses asks his question makes it clear, however, that he hopes to obtain God's distinct name. He wants a special name for God. The god of the Canaanites had the special name Baal, the god of the Babylonians was Bel, and the god of the Assyrians was Asshur. Moses was told that God's special name is *Yahweh.* We are sure of the four consonant sounds, so the name is sometimes referred to as the "tetragrammaton," that is "four letters." The vowels are less certain since the early Hebrew texts did not contain the vowels, but it is thought that the name would have been transliterated *Yahweh.*

In the postexilic period (after 538 B.C.), the Jews withdrew the sacred name from the popular pronunciation for fear it would be profaned. When the Massoretes added vowels to YHWH they used vowels from the word *adonai,* also translated "Lord." The Massoretes did their work in the sixth and seventh centuries A.D. The name Jehovah as applied to God is often attributed to Petrus Galatinus in A.D. 1520. The American Standard Version (1901) consistently uses this name, but the New American Standard Bible (1960), based on the ASV, dropped "Jehovah" and substituted "LORD." Therefore, a preference for addressing God as Jehovah has no biblical basis. If you wish to use the Hebrew special name for God, you should address him as "Yahweh."

Exodus clearly affirms God reveals his special name to Israel in Egypt at the time of the exodus.

> God (elohim) also spoke to Moses and said to him: "I am the LORD (Yahweh). I appeared to Abraham, Isaac, and Jacob as God Almighty (El shaddai), but by my name 'the LORD' I did not make myself known to them (Exod. 6:2).

The name "Yahweh" appeared earlier in the Old Testament, the first instance being Genesis 2:4. Genesis 4:26 has frequently been cited as an alternate claim in regard to the earliest instance of God being identified as *Yahweh,* and therefore it happened in the days of Seth rather than Moses. But perhaps the point of Genesis 4:26 is that in the days of Seth men first began to address God in prayer. The use of *Yahweh* therefore reflects the fact that even the earliest parts of Genesis were not written until *Yahweh* had revealed the tetragrammaton as his special name at the time of the exodus.

What is it that *Yahweh* makes known to his people at the time of the exodus? What is the significance of his special name? Some have taken *hayah* ("I am who I am") to refer to the eternity or essence of God. But this doesn't seem to be the intent of Exodus 3. God is of interest in the Old Testament not because of his eternal essence, but because he acts in the lives of his people in amazing ways. He is not so much the

God who stands above time but who enters into it. In fact, the NRSV supplies the alternate translation ("I will be what I will be"), which seems very attractive. This affirmation declares that Yahweh is known by his action. Man cannot confine God and proscribe his being. God's future is open. He is not boxed in by the Egyptians. He is not limited to his past actions. He will define himself by what he does, and what he will do in the future is not always immediately obvious. By what he did in Egypt with the plagues and at the sea, he proved his intent to fulfill his promise to Abraham. But the promise to Abraham did not reveal the amazing manner by which Yahweh would bring his people to the land. God's helping hand in Egypt was, of course, consistent with his promise. But what he did in Egypt shows that he is free to fulfill his promise in his own way. He will be what he will be!

A New Nation of Faith

Exodus clearly affirms that Yahweh was at work in the plagues in Egypt and at the Red Sea. What did God hope to accomplish in these actions? Exodus 1–18 shows that God had two purposes: (1) to create faith in his own people and (2) to convince the Egyptians and the nations of his might.

God exhibited many signs and wonders in Egypt to mold his people into a unified force. He desired a people who trusted him, who were ready to leave Egypt, and who would prepare in the wilderness for the war required so as to take the promised land. This was how God set out to bless these people, to fashion them into a nation so that they in turn would be a channel of blessing to the nations. These signs and wonders were not only for the first witnesses, but also for future generations. Faith would also arise in succeeding generations by these earlier wonders. Faith does not come easily, and, once achieved, it does not necessarily abide permanently. The Exodus story tells us that faith waxes and wanes even in the hearts of God's chosen people.

God launched many wonders to elicit faith. Moses said about the people, "But suppose they do not believe me or listen to me; but say, 'The LORD did not appear to you'" (Exod. 4:1). God supplied the power to turn a rod into a serpent, heal a leprous hand, and turn water into blood (Exod. 4:2-9). When Moses and Aaron arrived in Egypt, they performed these signs for the people. The result was faith (Exod. 4:31). Their faith, however, began to waver when Pharaoh refused Moses' request that the people be permitted to leave Egypt. Because of their audacious request, Pharaoh forced them to increase their brickmaking, while at the same time compounded the task by compelling them to gather their own straw. Israelite foremen laid the blame squarely at the feet of Moses and Aaron, and once again these leaders had reservations about following these men who claimed that Yahweh had appeared to them (Exod. 5:15-21). But God told Moses not to worry because the disdain of Pharaoh would supply him the occasion for working mighty wonders in Egypt (Exod. 6:1).

God therefore proceeded to exhibit his wondrous might. At the appropriate action of Moses, God turned water from the Nile River into blood; flooded Egypt with frogs, gnats, and flies; brought on them and their animals plagues and boils; sent hail, locusts, and darkness for three days; and finally slew the Egyptians' firstborn and their cattle (Exod. 7–11). The Hebrews looked on in great wonder. Their faith was obviously growing, but it became intense at the sea. Pharaoh finally and reluctantly agreed to let the people go when the firstborn of the land were lost. But on their way out of Egypt, Pharaoh once again changed his mind. As the people reached the region of the Red Sea, they could see dust ascending from Pharaoh's armies and chariots. Again, their fear of the Pharaoh grew and their faith in God failed (Exod. 14:10-12).

Moses spoke words of assurance and conviction. And Moses said to the people, "Do not be afraid, stand firm, and see the deliverance that the LORD will accomplish for you today; for the Egyptians whom you see today you shall never see again. The LORD will fight for you, and you have only to keep still" (Exod. 14:13-14). Moses was right. The sea opened, and they walked across to the other side on dry land. When the Egyptians followed, the waters returned and they were drowned. That was a mighty day, a great victory, and a moment of intense faith. "Israel saw the great work that the LORD did against the Egyptians. So the people feared the LORD and believed in the LORD and his servant Moses" (Exod. 14:31).

But even that faith did not last. After a few days in the wilderness, they became thirsty and commenced murmuring against Moses (Exod. 15:24). They grew hungry and murmured about the lack of food (Exod. 16:2). But God still had work to do, and out of this motley crew he created a nation of faith through whom he arranged to bless the nations.

These events were not only for people present then. They were for generations of future Israelites. Each year the Israelites were to reenact and remember those awesome times in the celebration of the Passover (Exod. 12:14). Faith was to be created in future generations by retelling the story. According to Deuteronomy 5:2-3:

> The LORD our God made a covenant with us in Horeb. Not with our ancestors did the LORD did make this covenant, but with us, who are all of us here alive today.

The celebration of the Passover introduced the oncoming generations to the mighty acts of God which laid the groundwork for the conviction of the Hebrews, that God led his oppressed people out of Egypt and gave them a land of their own to possess.

> When in the future your child asks you, 'What does this mean?' you
> shall answer, 'By strength of hand the LORD brought us out of Egypt,
> from the house of slavery' (Exod. 13:14).

It is common for young people to question why parents do what they do. Each of our five children wanted to know why we ate bits of bread and drank grape juice from the small cup. That was our chance to explain that certain past occurrences were so filled with reality that they explain and give direction to life even now.

Our age has turned its back on the past. It has more or less agreed with Henry Ford's famous comment, "What do we care what they did 500 or 1,000 years ago? . . . It means nothing to me. History is more or less bunk. It's tradition."[1] According to Exodus, the only way to make any sense out of the present is to learn what the God of the present and the future did in the past. By doing so, we find our identity in the present and face the future with confidence and expectation.

The mighty acts of God created a community of faith. The actions provided the base for the community's identity, and they bonded the community to reality. How can people who turn their backs on the past hope to locate any roots in reality? Reality encompasses the past, present, and the future.

The mighty acts of God are also three dimensional, growing out of the past, spreading into the present, and stretching into the future. In fact, the people of God don't make their own future, but they are drawn to it by the one who stands even in advance of the present. "And in the days of those kings the God of heaven will set up a kingdom that shall never be destroyed; nor shall this kingdom be left to another people. It shall crush all these kingdoms and bring them to an end, and it shall stand forever" (Dan. 2:44).

---

[1] John B. Rae, ed., *Henry Ford* (Englewood Cliffs, NJ: Prentice-Hall, 1969), pp. 53-54.

He Made the Nations Believers

As God affirmed in his promise to Abraham, his interests are wide reaching. Some gods might have a bad case of myopia, but not the Lord God of Israel. In what he did in Egypt and at the sea, Yahweh showed his desire not only to create a community of faith, but also to make believers out of the nations. Yahweh hoped to make known his ways to all men so they might share in his good gifts.

> When Pharaoh does not listen to you, I will lay my hand upon Egypt and bring my people the Israelites, company by company, out of the land of Egypt by great acts of judgment. The Egyptians shall know that I am the LORD, when I stretch out my hand against Egypt and bring the Israelites out from among them (Exod. 7:4-5).

Have you ever stopped to ask why ten plagues rather than just one? Or have you made any sense out of the fact that God hardened Pharaoh's heart (Exod. 10:20)? According to Exodus, the answer to both questions lies in the fact that Yahweh wanted all the nations to hear about these events. For that reason he multiplied the plagues. One plague might be passed off as a fluke. But not ten. In fact, the magicians of Pharaoh replicated the plagues through the third. But then admitted that they were badly outclassed by Moses and Aaron.

> The magicians tried to produce gnats by their secret arts, but they could not. There were gnats on both humans and animals. And the magicians said to Pharaoh, "This is the finger of God!" But Pharaoh's heart was hardened, and he would not listen to them, just as the LORD had said (Exod. 8:18-19).

> For this time I will send all my plagues upon you yourself, and upon your officials, and upon your people, so that you may know that there is no one like me in all the earth. For by now I could have stretched out my hand and struck you and your people with pestilence, and you would have been cut off from the earth. But this is why I have let you

live: to show you my power, and to make my name resound through
all the earth (Exod. 9:14-16).

Yahweh had just revealed his special name at the time of
the exodus. It was not widely known. But by his multifold
actions in Egypt, his name was on the lips of those who traveled to the outposts of civilization. God hardened Pharaoh's
heart so that the people would be forced to stay in Egypt.
God was simply confirming Pharaoh in his personal desires.
"I know, however, that the king of Egypt will not let you go
unless compelled by a mighty hand" (Exod. 3:19). God did
not change the course of Pharaoh's hopes or commitments.
In fact, Pharaoh played into the hand of God because of his
desire to retain the Israelites as slaves. Exodus does not
declare, in fact, that God hardened Pharaoh's heart until after
the sixth plague (Exod. 9:12). Up until that time, according
to the text, Pharaoh hardened his own heart.

By his mighty signs and wonders, God made a believing
nation out of the descendants of Jacob. Did he also achieve
his second purpose? That is, did he make believers out of the
nations? Yes! The great poetry in Exodus 15, which praises
Yahweh as a man of war, tells of the reaction of the nations.

> The peoples heard, they trembled; pangs seized the inhabitants of
> Philistia. Then the chiefs of Edom were dismayed; trembling seized the
> leaders of Moab; all the inhabitants of Canaan melted away. Terror
> and dread fell upon them; by the might of your arm, they became still
> as a stone until your people, O LORD, passed by, until the people whom
> You acquired passed by (Exod. 15:14-16).

Not only have the peoples of the Jordan valley heard,
but Jethro, Moses' father-in-law, was made a believer. When
a person impresses his father-in-law, that is something special.
When I first met my future wife, I soon found out my father-
in-law was not particularly fond of southerners or preachers.
He considered me a southerner even though I was born and
reared one mile north of the Mason-Dixon line in southern

Missouri. For that reason, any time I somehow impressed him, that was indeed a serendipity. The father-in-law of Moses was impressed. When he heard all that happened, he stated, "Now I know that the LORD is greater than all gods, because he delivered the people from the Egyptians, when they dealt arrogantly with them" (Exod. 18:11).

All of a sudden Yahweh's name, previously unknown to Jethro, zoomed past all the deities he had heard of before. Because of his belief, he "brought a burnt offering and sacrifices to God." The name of the Lord was indeed being declared throughout all the earth.

Rahab of Jericho best summed it up: "As soon as we heard it, our hearts melted, and there was no courage left in any of us because of you. The LORD your God is indeed God in heaven above and on earth below" (Josh. 2:11). Because of Rahab's faith and that of others, many persons were incorporated into the people of God.

All through the years in Egypt and in Israel's exodus, God showed his love for his people. His heart reached out to a cursed, enslaved people. He secured their release so he could shower his gifts upon them. And furthermore through them in order that the nations might know the name of Yahweh, take up his ways, and also bask in the warmth of his love.

Questions for Discussion

1. What do the earlier promises God made have to do with the exodus?

2. What do people need to do most of all so as to attain God's assistance?

3. What was the most important religious celebration for Israel? Why?

4. Why did Yahweh select Moses to free his people from the Egyptians?

5. What name did God, in response to Moses, give as his own special name? Why this name?

6. Is *Jehovah* God's special name? Why or why not?

7. Is "I am who I am" the most appropriate translation of *hayah*?

8. What did God hope to achieve in the plagues and in the exodus with Israel?

9. How does the celebration of the Passover continue to create a people of faith in Israel?

10. Why did God send ten plagues rather than just one?

11. Why was God so intent on the other nations believing?

12. Was it unfair for God to harden Pharaoh's heart?

5
Protection in the Wilderness

The Lord your God, who goes before you, is the one
who will fight for you, just as he did for you in Egypt
before your eyes, and in the wilderness, where you saw
how the Lord your God carried you, just as one carries a
child, all the way that you traveled until you reached this
place (Deut. 1:30-31).

The Israelites stood in the sand on the sun-kissed
banks of the Sinai Peninsula above the waters of the
Red Sea. Egypt lay to the west and behind. These newly liberated slave peoples faced northeast, toward the land promised as a gift to their progenitor almost 600 years previously, that is, to Abraham. God had redeemed his people, but a long trek lay ahead through the treacherous sand and stone of the wilderness before they could set foot in the land flowing with milk and honey. Even the most faithless did not anticipate just how long and disaster-ridden that journey would be. The time in the wilderness was not wasted, however, because it gave the people time to prepare for the days ahead. Above all, it was a time when the steadfast love of the Lord was explicitly manifest. In the wilderness, Yahweh daily showed how he loves to sustain his people.

According to the Preacher, there is a time for everything under the sun (Eccles. 3:1). There is even a time for preparation. For Israel, that time was the years spent in the wilderness, between the fleshpots of Egypt and the grapes and olives of Palestine. The preparation came from various experiences and on numerous fronts. It was often complex, perhaps even contradictory to people with small minds. But these same features characterize the preparation of a school-age child. Should the preparation of the people of Yahweh be less complex and time-consuming?

In the wilderness God accomplished many goals in regard to his relationship with Israel. That time in the life of the people was far more than just a time of punishment. As Israel prepared to enter the land, God was involved in: (1) preparation, (2) protection, (3) provision, (4) punishment, and (5) parenting. Underlying all these achievements was the conviction that God acted for the sake of his name.

Preparation

The route from the Red Sea to Palestine by "way of the land of the Philistines" was less than 200 miles. But that was not the way God directed his people (Exod. 13:17-18). The route he chose, even without detours and circumventions, was about 400 miles. Why did God send his people on such a circuitous journey? According to the text, the answer is preparation. The land they were to take would not fall without resistance. They had to be ready both mentally and physically.

Before Israel set out, they had an orderly and strategic plan for marching. The meeting tent was to be the center of the camp. Marching on the east were the tribes of Judah, Issachar, and Zebulun; on the south, Reuben, Simeon, and Gad; on the west, Ephraim, Manasseh, and Benjamin; and on the north, Dan, Asher, and Naphtali (Num. 2:1-34). The Levites were to be in the center surrounding the tent because it was their duty to transport and protect it (Num. 2:17). (This book will examine more detailed strategies for battles in chapter eight.) God does not send his people out unprepared. Among the ministries to which God calls his servants, the ministry of preparation is also included.

Protection

In many teaching contexts in synagogues and churches, the wilderness is identified as the place in which God punished his people. Of course, it was. Even New Testament texts emphasize that. "God was not pleased with most of them, and they were struck down in the wilderness" (1 Cor. 10:5). But much more than punishment occurred in the wilderness. In fact, God's people experienced the love of God and its implications in the wilderness. Yahweh protected his people as dearly beloved children even though at the same time they were being punished.

As we noted previously, God's love occurs first, and his wrath grows out of his love. So in the wilderness, punishment did not come before the love of God, but rather it was the result of it. Before God punished the people, he loved them freely. And because he loved them, he punished them for their waywardness in order to create the soil in which love could grow and become intense and permanent.

The Old Testament describes the love of God for his people in the wilderness in two manners: as the love of a father for his son, and as the love of a husband for his bride.

God loved to sustain his son, just as fathers love to provide the needs of their children.

> The LORD your God, who goes before you, is the one who will fight for you, just as he did for you in Egypt before your very eyes, and in the wilderness, where you saw how the LORD your God carried you, just as one carries a child, all the way that you traveled until you reached this place (Deut. 1:30-31).

Honest fathers, if they become desperate enough, will even steal in order to put food in the mouths of their children. In the wilderness, God protected and provided for his son even while punishing him. God gave his children water, manna, quail, a remedy for snakebite, and clothing (Deut. 29:1-6).

Can a father love and punish his son at the same time? According to the text, God did. But don't we too? And if we can do it, can't God do it even more?

Almost as soon as he could walk, my son liked to stray away from home without letting anyone know. We punished him in many different ways, but we never could get across to him the importance of our knowing where he was. When he was sixteen and had his driver's permit, he was gone for a couple of hours once, and we didn't know where he was. As a result, I told him he could not drive for a week. That was a bitter pill, but it made a point. We really wanted to know where he was. But even during his punishment we continued our love by sustaining him. He ate and drank as much as before, perhaps even more. In fact, while he was home, I taught him how to take off a mower blade and sharpen it.

So even in the midst of punishment, God continued to love and sustain his son. He protected them from every harm. Hosea's poetry says it vividly.

> Yet it was I who taught Ephraim to walk, I took them up in my arms; but they did not know that I healed them. I led them with cords of human kindness, with bands of love. I was to them like those who lift infants to their cheeks. I bent down to them and fed them (Hos. 11:3-4).

The prophets liked to characterize the wilderness as a place where God treated his people as a husband treats a bride. Jeremiah said the wilderness was a honeymoon time.

> Go and proclaim in the hearing of Jerusalem, Thus says the LORD: I remember the devotion of your youth, your love as a bride, how you followed me in the wilderness, in a land not sown. Israel was holy to the LORD, the first fruits of his harvest (Jer. 2:2-3a).

God loved his bride, and the bride returned the love. The bride, however, was not without guilt. Even during the honeymoon she proved faithless. "'All who ate of it were held guilty; disaster came upon them,' says the LORD" (Jer. 2:3b). Even a husband sometimes loves and punishes his bride at the same time.

Hosea and Ezekiel also talk about God's nuptial love for the people.

> Therefore, I will now allure her, and bring her into the wilderness, and speak tenderly to her. From there I will give her her vineyards, and make the Valley of Achor a door of hope. There she shall respond as in the days of her youth, as at the time when she came out of the land of Egypt (Hos. 2:14-15).

> I passed by you again and looked on you; you were at the age for love. I spread the edge of my cloak over you, and covered your nakedness: I pledged myself to you and entered into a covenant with you, says the Lord GOD, and you became mine (Ezek. 16:8).

God was preparing his people for intimate, divine love. Despite the punishment, the wilderness is a prime example of the fact that the "steadfast love of the LORD never ceases, his mercies never come to an end." God protected his wayward people, even those who didn't deserve it.

Provision

In the wilderness the people of Israel were without provisions. There was not enough water, so God provided from springs and rocks. There was no visible food supply and no economy to live on. God, however, provided manna from heaven. After awhile the people had had it up to here with manna. They murmured and complained, desirous of meat. And God brought quail into the camp on wings, riding the currents of the winds from the south.

> In the evening quails came up and covered the camp; and in the morning there was a layer of dew around the camp. When the layer of

> dew lifted, there on the surface of the wilderness was a fine flaky sub-
> stance, as fine as frost on the ground. When the Israelites saw it, they
> said to one another, "What is it?" For they did not know what it was.
> Moses said to them, "It is the bread that the LORD has given you to
> eat" (Exod. 16:13-15).

They had no raw materials from which to sew new clothing or shoes. But God provided. "The clothes on your back
did not wear out and your feet did not swell these forty
years" (Deut. 8:4).

Not only did God supply whatever Israel needed for sustenance, he guided them in the paths of his choosing through
a cloud by day and a pillar of fire by night. And finally when
they had constructed the tabernacle, he tented among them,
his glory being visible above the ark of the covenant. He was
their God, and they his people. Israel was abundantly blessed
by Yahweh's presence.

> Then the cloud covered the tent of meeting, and the glory of the
> LORD filled the tabernacle. Moses was not able to enter the tent of
> meeting because the cloud settled upon it, and the glory of the LORD
> filled the tabernacle. Whenever the cloud was taken up from the taber-
> nacle, the Israelites would set out on each stage of their journey; but
> if the cloud was not taken up, then they did not set out until the day
> that it was taken up. For the cloud of the LORD was on the tabernacle
> by day, and fire was in the cloud by night, before the eyes of all the
> house of Israel, at each stage of their journey (Exod. 40:34-38).

God provided these faithless and obstinate people with
whatever they needed. They did not deserve it. He freely gave
it in inexplicable love.

Punishment

Radical punishment is always a final resort with God.
God is not a motorcycle patrol officer, hiding behind the bill-
board, eager to trip up the unsuspecting. Yahweh did not
intend for his people to spend forty years in the wilderness.

But the situation became desperate as the result of so much murmuring and faithlessness until God exhausted all his options. The straw that broke the camel's back occurred soon after God gave his promise in covenant ("I will be their God and they will be my people"), and after the twelve spies, one from each tribe, had gone to search out the land. When they returned, ten said it was hopeless, but two believed that with God's help it could be done. All that night the people cried out and wept. They murmured against Moses and Aaron, and even proposed that new leaders be selected for a return to Egypt (Num. 14:1-12).

How could they be like that? They saw the power of God in Egypt and at the sea. They drank the water and ate the manna and quail. Now they had the audacity to complain that the challenge ahead was too great. What else could Yahweh do to convince them that no task was a challenge to Yahweh, maker of heaven and earth? They were a hopeless lot (Num. 14:11-12).

God did not carry out his threat, because Moses interceded. God is a God of mercy, so he pardoned the people. But he could not let such a faithless generation go scot-free.

> Nevertheless — as I live, and as all the earth shall be filled with the glory of the LORD — none of the people who have seen my glory and the signs that I did in Egypt and in the wilderness, and yet have tested me these ten times and have not obeyed my voice, shall see the land that I swore to give to their ancestors; none of those who despised me shall see it (Num. 14:21-23).

That generation did not get to enter the land. Those under twenty at that time, however, were eligible (14:29). The generations coming on, who grew up in the wilderness, were trained by God to enjoy the blessing of the land. The rejected generation had no real desire to be in close fellowship with God. They wanted to return to Egypt. God does not force humans. He gives them every opportunity. But if they persist in cultivating fellowship with the Egyptians rather than divine fellowship, then God permits ultimate separation from himself. So the older generation was punished, while the younger in effect was in boot camp training. The new generation was learning the ropes for occupying and living in the land they would ultimately inherit.

Parenting

Love relationships only grow where there is mutual trust. "[Love] bears all things, believes all things, hopes all things, endures all things" (1 Cor. 13:7). In the wilderness God disciplined his son Israel so that he would learn to trust him. Discipline comes in at least three varieties: (1) a training regimen to get ready for the battle or the big game, (2) obstacles placed in the path to bring a person to his or her senses, and (3) drastic punishment when all other avenues have been exhausted. Yahweh used all these means of discipline, but in the text it is specifically the first (a training regimen) which is called discipline. Deuteronomy sees the wilderness as a time of discipline. "Know then in your heart that as a parent disciplines a child so the LORD your God disciplines you" (Deut. 8:5). The eighth chapter begins with the admonition to scrupulously obey all of God's commands. The reason for keeping the commandments — so things will go well for them in the promised land — is the major theme of Deuteronomy (Deut. 8:1,19-20; 6:3).

Discipline by Training

What then is the point of the discipline in the wilderness? God is putting his people through a regimen so they will come out trusting his commandments. Deuteronomy 8:2 says, "Remember the long way that the LORD your God has led you these forty years in the wilderness, in order to humble you, testing you to know what was in your heart, whether or not you would keep His commandments." What method will God employ to achieve this end? He will humble his people. But how will that prepare them for keeping his commandments? The way he humbled them was to make them utterly dependent on him.

Every parent with teenagers or anyone who has been a teenager knows what a humbling experience it is to be totally dependent on parents for spending money. Along with the money comes a felt obligation to demonstrate deference to the person from whom it came. But once the teenager makes his own money, he feels he has the right to do with it as he pleases.

God first of all put his people in circumstances in which they were totally dependent on him for sustenance. "He humbled you by letting you hunger, then by feeding you with manna, with which neither you nor your ancestors were acquainted" (8:3a). The people had to depend on God for food. They learned he was trustworthy. They didn't have to worry about the manna. They could count on it. When God supplied manna, he didn't have to get up at 3:00 a.m., fire up the ovens, knead the dough, put it in the cutter, then into the ovens. He simply said, "Let there be manna." In a figurative sense, manna came from the mouth of God. So the writer says, "in order to make you understand that one does not live by bread alone; but by every word that comes from the mouth of the LORD" (8:3b). God's people learned to trust manna that came from the mouth of God. And they should likewise trust the commandments of God and obey them, for they also came from his mouth.

In the last part of chapter eight the author makes it obvious that when the Israelites get to the land and they have produced their own crops and gathered the fruit from the vineyards, they will be tempted to think they earned it themselves. They may think they no longer need to pay any deference to Yahweh by obeying his commandments (Deut. 8:11-14).

In the wilderness God trained his son for the day when he would occupy the promised land. To prosper in the land, he had to keep God's commandments, ordinances, and statutes. Israel was between Egypt and the land promised. We too are in the wilderness between the resurrection of Jesus Christ and our own resurrection. In this wilderness God also disciplines us. When we become convinced that we created our own talents and we ignore his demands, he humbles us to teach us that for things to go well we must trust everything that comes from God's mouth — his demands as well as his blessings. We too relish the health, wealth, and wisdom that come from God. They all come from his mouth, because that is the singular source of his gifts. We too, then need to learn that his commandments are good because they have exactly the same source — the mouth of God.

Discipline by Obstacles

God also disciplines by putting obstacles in the way of his people. Amos makes this obvious. In the middle of the eighth century BC the Northern Kingdom under Jeroboam II was doing exceedingly well politically and economically, but the poor were suffering. Amos came from the south with the message that their prosperity would be short-lived if they did not develop a heart of compassion for the needy. Amos insisted that God had been working with them through the years to develop justice and righteousness toward all the inhabitants of the land. But he had little success. He first of all gave them cleanness of teeth, meaning drought, hoping it would bring them to their senses and they would return. But it didn't faze them (Amos 4:6). Next he sent blight and mildew to waste their crops. But the results were the same. "Yet you did not return to me," says the Lord. He sent pestilence, and he sent enemy troops. But nothing worked. So drastic punishment remained. "Prepare to meet your God, O Israel!" (Amos 4:12).

Discipline by Drasrtic Punishment

God loves his people so much he will do anything in keeping with love to restore them to his fellowship when they drift away. He will deprive them to help them learn to trust him for their needs. He will even let some seemingly harmful incident occur if it brings them to their senses. Injuries do not seem to be acts of love, but they may be so indeed when aimed at restoring relationships.

> Come, let us return to the Lord; for it is he who has torn, and he will heal us; he has struck down, and he will bind us up. After two days he will revive us; on the third day he will raise us up, that we may live before him (Hos. 6:1-2).

Hosea suggests that sometimes the only way God can make our life better is by tearing something.

When I was five, my uncle, who had learned gymnastics in college, in flipping me from his feet in order to do a somersault, threw me into a tree. The result was that I came up with a broken arm. In those depression years in southern Missouri, no X-ray equipment was available. The doctor set the arm, then applied wooden splints, gauze, and plaster. In four weeks the big day arrived for removing the splint. If the arm was straight, there would be great relief. But if the arm was crooked, there would be only one thing to do: break it again and reset it. Fortunately this did not have to be done in my case, but had it been necessary, it would have been preferable to the opposite consequence. Breaking an arm does not seem like an act of love, but in the long run it is more desirable than a crooked arm. Who wants to go around with a crooked arm the rest of one's life?

To God, it is more desirable to break a life than let it grow crooked. "He has torn, that he may heal us." Unfortunately, in a number of cases the tearing makes no appreciable difference. After numerous tries, each resulting in failure, the only alternative is "prepare to meet your God." Yahweh's love is so steadfast that he never gives up. He is continually at work preparing his children and struggling to bring them back when they drift away.

God Acts for His Name's Sake

While Moses was on the mountain receiving the law, the people worshiped the golden calf that they fabricated in the fire. The calf symbolized Baal, the god of the Canaanites (Exod. 32:1-6). God grew distraught and threatened to wipe them out. Later, when the people threatened to select new leaders and go back to Egypt, God again determined to consume them. In each case, Moses argued with God and brought about a repentance. It seems strange that a human could explain certain facts of life to God and win him over. But according to the text, that is what actually happened. Moses argued that it was in God's best interest to continue with the people, however faithless and rebellious, not just for their own sake, but because of how the action of Yahweh would appear to the nations looking on. Moses appealed to God to act for the sake of his name.

What does it mean for God to act for the sake of his name? "He leads me in right paths for his name's sake" (Ps. 23:3).

The sequence of events are similar in the Exodus 32 incident and in Numbers 13–14, after the spies argued that the land could not be conquered. First, God became upset because his people spurned his love. The description of the anger of God reminds one of the anguish of a married person who has just happened upon a spouse in the embrace of a lover.

> The LORD said to Moses, "I have seen this people, how stiff-necked they are. Now let me alone, so that my wrath may burn hot against them and I may consume them; and of you I will make a great nation" (Exod. 32:9-10).

In Western philosophy we have been led to believe that such personal characteristics cannot really be attributed to God. But the God of the philosophers is not the God of the Bible. The God of the Bible is as personal as a human being is personal because man is made in God's image. God has the traits of a person, though God's attributes far exceed those of a human. God is a loving God, but his love is so intense that when his lover deceives him, he suffers just as a human. The author of Exodus has no qualms about depicting God as jealous. "For you shall worship no other god, because the LORD, whose name is Jealous, is a jealous God" (Exod. 34:14).

Love involves freedom — freedom to love or not to love. Coercion is not love. But freedom also involves risk because the advances of the lover may be rejected. Rejected love brings on hurt, burning, suffering, and wrath. Therefore, despite the traditional Christian theology that rejects the suffering of God and affirms his impassability, the God of the Old Testament suffers. He does not deteriorate; he does not dissipate. But he suffers because he loves. In both cases, God suffered as the result of the rejected love from his beloved. Yahweh was especially hurt that Israel attributed his caring actions to Baal, the god of the Canaanites.

> They have been quick to turn aside from the way that I commanded them; they have cast for themselves an image of a calf, and have worshiped it and sacrificed to it, and said, "These are your gods, O Israel, who brought you up out of the land of Egypt!" (Exod. 32:8).

God Apprehends the Human Perspective

Second, Moses argued with God and changed the expressed intentions of God. In Exodus, Moses used two arguments: (1) that the Egyptians would accuse God of malice and lose respect for him, and (2) God should remember his promise to Abraham, Isaac, and Israel. In Numbers, Moses argued that (1) the nations would question the power of

Yahweh if his people died in the wilderness, and (2) Yahweh is a God of steadfast love, slow to anger, and forgiving.

How can we account for the fact that Moses was able to change the decision of God? Moses actually did not put any new ideas into the mind of God, as if he were brighter or more perceptive than God. He only pointed out an idea or commitment that came from God in the first place. God had told Moses that through his actions he sought to declare his name throughout the earth (Exod. 9:16). God had promised Abraham numerous descendants (Gen. 22:16,18). And God had declared to Moses on the mountain that he was a God of steadfast love and forgiveness (Exod. 34:6-7).

Moses was not putting ideas into the mind of God but reminding God of the commitments he himself had made. Therefore, the arguments of Moses did not change God, they merely revised his specific course of action. Some might still be surprised, but Christians should be the least so. This says that God has always been interested in how things look from the human perspective.

God sent his Son in human form as another clear indication that he wants to know what it is like from the human perspective. Before God sent his son he did not know what it was like to live as a human.

When my daughter told me she wanted to go away from Abilene to college, she said one thing, which was cutting at first. She said, "You don't really understand why I want to go away because you don't know what it's like to be the daughter of Tom Olbricht and be a student at the college where he teaches." That hurt. I first thought, "Why that ungrateful wretch. What does she mean I don't know what it is like to be Tom Olbricht's daughter?" I saw her when she took her first step. I remembered when she told me she had learned to rest on her first day in kindergarten. I remembered her first date. I knew more about her than she did herself. But after I cooled down a bit, I realized she was right. I knew many things about her, things she did not know herself. But I did not know the experience of being my own daughter and attending the college where I taught. So I grudgingly said to her, "I guess you're right. I don't know what it's like. Tell me and perhaps I will be able to think about it in a new perspective."

God, also did not have the experience of what it was like to be his child. To have that experience, he came into the world as human, that is the Son. And now the Son is seated on the right hand of God, constantly explaining to God what it is like to be human (Heb. 4:14-16). God seeks the human perspective. That is what prayer is about. When prayers remind God of his commitment and show that if he acts in a certain way in this situation it will be in line with his commitments, then we can expect prayer to have an effect on the action of God.

God's Name Is Cleared

Third, as a result of God's action, his people came off better than they deserved because God's name was at stake. Ezekiel tells of the continual rebellion of the Israelites against God. But after reflecting upon the situation, God did not destroy them (Ezek. 20:8-9).

God's people always come off better than they deserve because they wear the name of God. But if they drag the name of God through the mud and thereby profane his name, God will act against his people to clear his name (Jer. 14:1-10). This action of God is not a separate characteristic of God from love. God has made a commitment to love all of his created order forever. Whenever any person tries to corner all God's love, God will resist. When God loves, it does not imply that he hurries to comply with every human request. In this text, when God acts for the sake of his name, he acts in consideration for all inhabitants of the earth. According to the Old Testament, the self-interest of God is the equitable treatment of all those who bear his image.

Finally, in each case God did not destroy his people on the spot, but neither did he let them off easily. Exodus 32:25-29 says those who did not line up with God were slain, and the faithless in Numbers 14:20-38 were sentenced to spend their life in the wilderness and never occupy the land God promised to Abraham. What God did in the wilderness shows us, if nothing else, exactly how amazingly relentless his love is. We grow more and more amazed at the amount of attention he gives to drawing man to himself in intimate fellowship. The wilderness period is a wonderful account of how Yahweh the God of Israel and the father of the Lord Jesus Christ struggles daily with his wayward, but beloved people.

Questions for Discussion

1. Why did Israel need time for preparation before entering the land?

2. In what ways did God protect Israel in the wilderness?

3. Can God achieve more than one end at a time in a series of events?

4. In what ways did Yahweh provide for his people in the wilderness?

5. Who were the people more specifically punished in the wilderness?

6. Can people who at one time experience the mighty power of God later have a failure of nerve?

7. How is humbling a disciplining?

8. What is the implication of Deuteronomy 8 that everything that comes from the mouth of God is good?

9. What might be going on when God's people experience "tearing"?

10. Did Moses change God's very being by his arguments? What did he change?

11. What is meant by God's acting for the sake of his name?

12. Do we fare better than we sometimes deserve, as did Israel?

6
Promise through the Covenants

We live in a world of eroding commitment. Sometimes it seems like promises are made to be broken. Commitments to personal relationships are easily forgotten. A person's word is no longer his or her bond. We seldom hear praise for long-standing loyalty to one position, one institution, one corporation, one spouse, one service club, or one church.

However, Yahweh, God of Israel, loved commitment. He loved to make promises that would commit him forever. He thrived on permanent relationships. He didn't hesitate to put his promises in writing. He continually made covenant promises to his people. Yahweh was not one to reserve the privilege of changing his mind tomorrow. He freely entered into covenant relationships with his people that were to extend into perpetuity.

> I will establish my covenant between me and you and your offspring after you throughout their generations, for an everlasting covenant, to be God to you and to your offspring after you (Gen. 17:7).

The Promise to Noah

The word covenant first occurs in the Old Testament in the promises to Noah (Gen. 6:18). God once thought to rid his creation of perverse humankind. But he relented and instead promised Noah, "I establish my covenant with you, that . . . never again shall there be a flood to destroy the earth" (Gen. 9:11). God's promise to Noah was much like Saul's to Jonathan (1 Sam. 19:6). Saul who had kingly authority, made a promise to his son. The promise bound only Saul, "As the LORD lives, he shall not be put to death" (1 Sam. 19:6). A greater person committed himself to a lesser one. And Saul didn't demand any action or commitment in return. So, Yahweh, the emperor of the universe, made a personal promise to Noah. By this commitment he affirmed the nature of his future actions and tied his own hands. In a beautiful statement he committed himself to faithfulness in regard to creation. "As long as the earth endures, seedtime and harvest, cold and heat, summer and winter, day and night, shall not cease" (Gen. 8:22).

It is consequential that God's promise to Noah, to every living creature, and to all future generations, depended solely upon his goodness (Gen. 9:12). Unlike our contracts (covenants) in which the party of the first part agrees to sell a house to a party of the second part in exchange for a stated sum of money, God entered into an agreement with the created order but did not exact anything in return. God did not require an action from Noah to either inaugurate or maintain the covenant. Although prior to the covenant he laid charges on him, they had no bearing on the covenant (Gen. 9:1-7). Nothing was conditional about the Noachian covenant.

God promised that the earth would never again be destroyed by a flood. As a sign that he would never again destroy humankind, Yahweh set his bow in the sky. Man had nothing to do but enjoy the grace and goodness of God in his promise, which will continue regardless of what man does. Our existence does not teeter on the abyss. We are not so threatened that every moment hangs by a thread. We know that as long as the earth lasts we are secure from the primordial waters.

The Promise to Abraham

When Yahweh decided upon a new manner in which to share his goodness with creation, he called a man named Abraham. Through him God intended to bless the nations. Abraham's relationship with God resulted from God's initiative, not Abraham's. Abraham probably served other deities until called. "Long ago your ancestors — Terah and his sons Abraham and Nahor — lived beyond the Euphrates and served other gods" (Josh. 24:2). But when the call came, Abraham responded. God promised Abraham that his descendants would be as numerous as the stars (Gen. 15:5) and that he would give him the land (15:17-21). Neither of these promises were Abraham's by natural right; they were gifts of God because of his love.

The account of the ratification of God's covenant with Abraham may be puzzling until certain features are explained. To declare our commitment to a contract, we merely sign it in the presence of a notary public. The ratification of an ancient covenant was much more complicated. Animals were killed and halves of the carcasses were placed over against each other (Gen. 15:7-11; Jer. 34:18). Then the parties to the covenant passed through the halves to signify their approval.

Once Abraham had prepared the animals as instructed, "a smoking fire pot and a flaming torch passed between these pieces" (Gen. 15:17). This gave notice that Yahweh, though unseen, passed through the halves to ratify the covenant. We aren't told that Abraham also passed through the halves. Only God had to ratify the covenant since he alone launched it and kept it in force.

Obviously God gave many specific commands to Abraham. He asked him to leave his homeland, take Isaac to the mountain as a sacrifice, and walk before him and be blameless. But God extended the promise to Abraham before he made these demands. Therefore, the covenant did not depend upon Abraham's obedience but upon the grace and love of Yahweh. The sign of God's promise to Abraham was circumcision (Gen. 17:11), which could be seen as a work demanded by God and upon which the covenant was conditioned. But the sign was worked upon the recipient. It was not the work of the one circumcised.

Some argue that a later covenant rescinds the authority of an earlier one. The covenant with Abraham, however, did not cancel God's promise to Noah. In fact, the promise to Abraham built on the covenant with Noah. God capitalized upon his commitment to Noah and his descendants that he would treat the earth as inviolable, by his new declaration that through Abraham he would bless the nations. God thereby set out to share his goodness with man to whom he had already guaranteed an extended existence. He carefully laid his plans from one covenant to another, demonstrating his undying love by the cumulative benefits.

The Promise to David

The promise to David supplied additional layers to the oral commitments of God. God promised Noah that the earth and its people would be around for an incredibly long time. He promised Abraham he would raise up a people through whom mankind would be blessed. God added to the stability of his people by declaring that a seed of David would always reign on the throne in Jerusalem. Once God launches a plan or makes a commitment he sees it through. His love is forever.

The covenant with David followed the pattern of the promises to Noah and Abraham. First, the covenant was launched by the grace of God freely given. David declared to God that he would build him a house, that is, a temple for worship (2 Sam. 7). But God countered that he would act before David had a chance. Second, only God made the commitment. He did not call upon David or his descendants to do anything to secure the promise. There was nothing conditional: "Your throne shall be established forever" (2 Sam. 7:16). Regardless of what David or his descendants do, the covenant will stand. Third, the covenant with David was not only for David but also for his descendants and ultimately all persons (Isa. 11:10). However, unlike the covenants with Noah and Abraham, no sign is mentioned this time. Although the initial clause of the covenant with David is unconditional, a conditional aspect exists in regard to individual kings. "When he commits iniquity, I will punish him with a rod such as mortals use" (2 Sam. 7:14). God will not tolerate any foolishness or insubordination from the kings. If a king is faithless, he will be deposed. But the dynasty of David will not cease; a new seed will be elevated to the throne. Each king is to be judged according to the Mosaic covenant (Ps. 89:29-32). The blessing of God and his grace didn't come about as a consequence of the king's works. Yahweh had already promised his love and gave it freely. The blessing of God is not the result of human action or work. The keeping of the Mosaic rules did not secure God's favor, but indeed many a king triggered the removal of God's blessing by turning his back on Yahweh's rules. The doors of heaven are never opened because of the works of men, but they are closed whenever man fails to obey the demands of God.

In examining the covenants with Noah, Abraham, and David, we notice certain verities. First, God, though superior to humankind, bound himself in covenant, not out of necessity, but out of love. Second, in these three cases the promises were unilateral. God made a promise but did not ask anything in return. Third, each promise built on preceding ones, rather than canceling them. Fourth, God's covenants or promises always remain in force regardless of what man does or does not do. By his action, man can cut himself off from the benefits of the covenant, but the covenant remains as long as God decrees. God's promises are forever because his love is forever.

The Covenants as Unmerited Love

The Old Testament speaks of many mutual covenants such as those between Isaac and Abimelech (Gen. 26:31), Jonathan and David (1 Sam. 18:3), and Jacob and Laban (Gen. 31:44-54). But no covenant given by God is a mutual covenant. Who could consider himself equal with God to presume initiating a mutual covenant?

I have a mutual contract with a savings bank for a house mortgage. If the bank withdraws the money, the contract will be broken. If I stop making payments, the contract will be voided. But even if Israel stopped making its "payments," all the covenants would remain. God initiated the covenants, and only he can withdraw them. When people made covenants with God, they did not presume mutuality — they did not lay claims on God. Instead, they committed themselves to live according to the covenant which God had made (2 Chr. 34:31). Their covenant was to keep the "commandments, testimonies and statutes" — language depicting the Deuteronomic covenant and law.

Too often we think our relationship with God depends as much on what we have done as on what he has done. But the covenants of the Old Testament tell us that we are in this relationship because of what God has done. All we do is reach out and receive it.

About twenty years ago I heard a sermon developed from the following equation written on a blackboard: Salvation = God's Part + Man's Part. The preacher did not explain exactly what God's part was, only what man had to do. Perhaps it was not the preacher's intention, but we got the impression that man's part is at least as significant as God's. Salvation was presented as a fifty-fifty arrangement. But in the Old Testament redemption is never fifty-fifty. God gave covenants out of his good graces. Man simply received what God gave.

When I taught at Pennsylvania State University in the 1960s, the Hershey Foundation of Hershey, PA, gave Penn State $50 million to build a medical school. Newspaper articles told about the foundation and its benevolence through the years. Pictures showed the president of the foundation presenting the president of Penn State a check for $50 million. Nothing was said about what Eric Walker, president of Penn State, had to do to receive the check. The magnificent gift of the foundation far overshadowed anything the president did.

And so it is with the magnificent gift God offers to every man and woman made in his image. His gift is fellowship — a permanent relationship with him. This relationship is not a combination of God's part and man's part. In the words of the Christian hymn, "Jesus paid it all." But once the gift is received, God's people must live worthy of it, just as Penn State had much to do once it accepted the magnificent gift. In two years a medical school began taking shape.

The Mosaic Covenant

As the day approached for Israel to be a mighty nation, God gave his people a covenant in order to bond them into a nation living under rules and regulations. According to ancient analogies, in this act Yahweh was like a mighty emperor extending a treaty to a small and helpless nation. Through his mighty loving deeds God earned the right to bind this nation to himself. He had every reason to expect the people to honor his demands.

The Old Testament covenants followed the standard forms of the times. God has always shown his concern by communicating with humans in their own language. The late A.D. Nock, a Harvard professor, told the story about the little old lady in Boston who, at 80, began studying Hebrew so she could speak to her maker in his own language. However, the Old Testament teaches the opposite. God did not teach man his own language. Rather man himself named all living creatures (Gen. 2:19-20). The ultimate revelation, the Son, was clothed in human flesh. "The Word became flesh and lived among us" (John 1:14).

The Mosaic covenant, in structure if not in concept, is much like the ancient suzerainty treaty which nations utilized in the days of Moses. In a suzerainty treaty, a powerful ancient emperor (suzerain) extended a covenant to a small vassal state on his border. Before offering a covenant, he befriended the smaller country, often by defending it against a large power. After he successfully defeated the enemy, he drew up a covenant and offered it to the smaller nation. He did not enter the relationship as a partner, but as a concerned superior. He did not ask the small nation to contribute its ideas as to what should be included.

In the covenant, the suzerain promised to protect the small country. In return, he expected faithful allegiance to specific stipulations spelled out in the document. He concluded the arrangement by declaring blessings upon the small nation if it faithfully abided by its oath to uphold the covenant, and curses if it violated the stipulations. In concept, the Mosaic covenant was much like the suzerainty treaty. Yahweh was a sovereign Lord who befriended a small band of people enslaved in Egypt. He acted powerfully and benevolently for the Israelites by breaking the shackles of the Egyptian overlord. He eventually made them a nation in their own right. In the wilderness, where they set up camp, he extended his covenant. He did so out of love, not because of anything they had done (Deut. 7:6-12). "It was because the LORD loved you" (vs. 8). In the covenant he promised to be their God, guiding, loving and protecting as he did in Egypt (Deut. 4:37-39). In return, he expected them to fulfill his ways as stipulated in statutes and laws (4:39-40; 5:1-21). Unlike the covenants with Noah and Abraham, God expected his people to ratify the covenant, and he laid out specific laws for them to keep.

The Mosaic covenant included works for the people to fulfill — works of the law. But we need to understand that in context. The people of Israel did not receive the covenant because of who they were or what they had done.

> It was not because you were more numerous than any other people that the LORD set His heart on you and chose you — for you were the fewest of all peoples. It was because the LORD loved you and kept the oath that he swore to your ancestors, that the LORD has brought you out with a mighty hand, and redeemed you from the house of slavery, from the hand of Pharaoh king of Egypt (Deut. 7:7,8).

Neither was it because they were deserving or righteous.

> Know, then, that the LORD your God is not giving you this good land to occupy because of your righteousness; for you are a stubborn people. Remember and do not forget how you provoked the LORD your God to wrath in the wilderness; you have been rebellious against the LORD from the day you came out of the land of Egypt until you came to this place (Deut. 9:6,7).

God freely offered his covenant out of love. Israel did not keep the covenant in force by observing the law. The covenant remained because God loves to bless his people (Deut. 5:29; 6:24). As modern persons so often do, Israel cut itself off from God's blessings by failing to uphold its part

(Deut. 8:19-20). The sign of the Mosaic covenant was the sabbath (Exod. 31:17). God gave the sabbath. Man showed his support of the covenant by keeping the sabbath. The Mosaic covenant added to the promise to Abraham because God gave rules to the nation descended from Abraham.

The Relationship as a Marriage Covenant

The prophets compared the relationship between God and his people to the marriage bond or covenant. Yahweh is obviously the husband and Israel the wife. Yahweh wanted his wife to be faithful and loyal to the marriage vows. "I will take you for my wife in faithfulness" (Hos. 2:20). But when his bride sought out the gods of other nations, she exhibited her unfaithfulness, playing the harlot (Exod. 34:13-16).

The marriage relationship is the most compelling, intense companionship known by humans. The prophets used this analogy because they believed the most profound relationship a person could enter was with God. Anyone who thwarts the divine-human relationship can expect the same wrath and fury given a wife who spends her time in the bed of lovers.

Hosea, Ezekiel, and Jeremiah especially depict wayward Israel as Yahweh's faithless wife. The use of the husband-wife analogy presupposes that God's rapprochement with his people is not simply a legal one, but a relationship of love in which promises are made to reserve oneself for the lover. Of course, marriage also has legal aspects, but the motivation to enter the contract grows out of love.

Hosea hammered out his theology from the crisis of his own marriage. He married a woman named Gomer who later sought other lovers. Hosea still loved her despite her infidelity, and he continually sought to restore her to himself. Yahweh did likewise with Israel, his unfaithful bride (Hos. 2:6-15). Just as Hosea was willing to take back his harlot wife, so Yahweh desired the return of his wife. He was willing to take her back, no questions asked, but not without strings attached. "You must remain as mine for many days; you shall not play the whore, you shall not have intercourse with a man; nor I with you" (Hos. 3:3). Because of God's steadfast love for his bride, he tried everything to gain her back. "Come, let us return to the LORD; for it is he who has torn, and he will heal us" (Hos. 6:1).

Ezekiel used the marriage analogy in several places, especially chapters 16 and 23. Chapter 16 describes Israel as a young girl who, unwanted by her parents, is left exposed in an open field (v. 5). But God took her, cleaned her, and entered into a pledge of marriage with her (16:8). God was a very loving, affectionate husband (16:10-14). But Israel was not content with the love of God. "But you trusted in your beauty, and played the whore because of your fame, and lavished your whorings on any passer-by" (16:15). Israel's lust was so strong that there was no discrimination whatsoever used in seeking out lovers (16:31-34). Israel's harlotry involved worshiping the gods of other peoples and building altars to them (16:23-29). Because of such unfaithfulness, Yahweh threatened to expose Israel's lewdness to her neighbors by letting her enemies overrun the country (16:39). The separation, however, would not be permanent. God still loved his bride and planned to take her back through an everlasting covenant (16:60).

Jeremiah employed the same analogy in chapters 2–5. He pictured Israel sneaking away to her illicit lover through worship at the Baal shrines on the high places (Jer. 2:20-22). He charged that the passion for worshiping Baal was so strong that it was just like a female animal in heat (2:24). "Who can restrain her lust?" But since Yahweh was a God of mercy, he continually tried to woo back his wayward wife (3:11-14; 4:1-4).

The New Covenant

Because of Israel's perennial unfaithfulness, the prophets expected God to usher in a new age and change human hearts so as to cure their harlotry. Certain prophets spoke of a new covenant. The existing covenant and law were not inferior. The problem was man, the covenant breaker.

Hosea was among the earliest to herald a new day. According to Hosea, God will betroth his people to himself in faithfulness (Hos. 2:20). The covenant of which Hosea speaks fails to propose a new set of laws, but it envisions a change of relationships between animals, man, and God (Hos. 2: 18). In the new day, the law of God will be written on the heart (Jer. 31:33), implying not so much a new law, but a new manner in which the law is to empower life.

The new covenant does not annul prior covenants, but renders them efficacious for human existence. Ezekiel also speaks of a new covenant (Ezek. 34:25). In the day of the new covenant humans will be so reconstituted that they can keep the covenant. They will have a new heart (36:26), and a new spirit, which will be God's spirit (36:27).

Questions for Discussion

1. What sort of God binds himself to a peoples in writing?

2. Is the covenant of God with Noah a covenant between equals?

3. Will any belief or action on the part of Noah or other creatures render the covenant null and void?

4. What is the significance of the smoking fire pot and the flaming torch?

5. Did David or his descendants have to do anything to obtain God's promise of an everlasting dynasty?

6. Can human action destroy or nullify a divine covenant?

7. Does salvation = God's part + man's part?

8. In what ways is the Mosaic covenant similar to an ancient political treaty?

9. In what manner could God's people break the Mosaic covenant?

10. Is there any sense in which the Mosaic covenant is conditional?

11. Why did the prophets characterize Israel as a faithless bride?

12. Will the new covenant of Jeremiah cancel the stipulations of the Mosaic covenant?

7
Love through the Law

*B*ecause of God's steadfast love, he gives rules. Now that's interesting. In fact, it seems just paradoxical. Why would someone who loves even want to give laws? After all, love and law are opposite, aren't they? But is it just possible that if love lasts it has to be based on law?

When my oldest daughter was eight she decided she wanted to be a doctor. As a junior in high school she met a senior who also planned a medical career. They went to different colleges, but their romance blossomed. They soon began discussing plans for marriage. Without rules, however, the relationship probably would never have worked out. Since he was a year ahead of Suzanne, the first decision involved which medical school to attend. The rule was that he apply to a medical school with an inclination to accept females. The second rule was that preferably the school have a three-year program including summers so they could graduate at the same time. Fortunately, they discovered a school that met both criteria — Baylor Medical College. After three years the day approached when they would graduate. Then they looked for a place to do their residency. They required a hospital with a record for appointing husbands and wives and giving them essentially the same schedule so they could have some time together. After considerable checking they found in Boston City Hospital such a place. Because of the many hours involved in residency, it is difficult to see how the relationship could have lasted without these rules.

God loves to give rules so his people will be in a continual and rewarding relationship with him. Without rules they simply drift about, not benefiting from a growing, loving relationship. "Then the Lord commanded us to observe all these statutes, to fear the LORD our God, for our lasting good, so as to keep us alive, as is now the case" (Deut. 6:24).

Law and Love

The loving action of God is obvious throughout the Old Testament. Even the law is a result of the love of God. God called Abraham out of love, then gave him various commands to follow so that he would be blessed and through him the nations also be blessed. Later, God led the descendants of Abraham out of Egypt and through the wilderness and there offered his covenant. He extended his covenant because of his love, not as the consequence of their worth. He entered into a covenant because he was willing to commit himself forever.

Law is an integral part of the covenant. After God announced what he had lovingly done for his people, he gave them a list of rules to live by (Exod. 20:2-17). Political covenants in the ancient world commenced with benevolent actions of a strong nation for a weaker nation. Loving actions precede the covenant offer. Since the covenant results from the loving kindness of God and since law is an integral part of the covenant, law itself is grounded in the love of God.

Sometimes we see law as obstructive, harsh, and impersonal. For example, I may want to build a high-rise apartment building in a residential section of town, but a local zoning law prevents it. The zoning law is obstructive because it presents a barrier to what I want to do. Consider the case of a Texas man who went to prison because he committed three minor offenses. His sentence was executed under the state "habitual offender" law. The severity of the law in this instance shocks us. Then there are the impersonal traffic laws. Suppose the speed limit is 55 miles per hour, but we are in a hurry and decide to go 60 mph. We do not really believe we are infringing on anyone's rights or hurting anyone. It is so impersonal. We feel no demands of love. If we obey the law, it is simply because we believe in toeing the line exactly, are afraid of being fined, or are economy minded.

It is difficult to see how God's law could be obstructive, harsh, or impersonal. It was created from the deep recesses of his love. Christians sometimes envision the Old Testament sacrifices as obstructive. Perhaps we have misread the New Testament. The Hebrews writer, for example, does not think the sacrifices are obstructive, just inadequate when compared with the sacrifice of Christ (Heb. 9:26-28). The Israelites felt a joyful release through sacrifice.

> Now my head is lifted up above my enemies all around me, and I will offer in his tent sacrifices with shouts of joy; I will sing and make melody to the LORD (Ps. 27:6).

The sacrifices may have been stopgap, but they were the best forgiveness available. For that reason, they broke forth in unconstrained joy.

Some rules in the Old Testament seem harsh, such as those concerning an obstinate son (Deut. 21:18-21). Despite how it may strike us, such a law was common in the ancient Near East in lieu of a prison system. Human communities find it extremely difficult to function with exceptionally disruptive persons who roam about doing as they wish. Ancient humans exuberantly praised the law of God because they believed it protected them from dangers lurking on all sides. The law of a loving, caring God must be praiseworthy.

> Oh, how I love your law! It is my meditation all day long. . . . How sweet are your words to my taste, sweeter than honey to my mouth! . . . Your decrees are my heritage forever; they are the joy of my heart (Ps. 119:97,103,111).

Least of all could Israel look upon the law of God as impersonal. God's mighty loving acts preceded his law. The violation of his law was therefore a personal affront to God. It was to bite the hand that fed it. To disobey a law of God is not simply to break the law of the land. It is to infringe upon a loving relationship.

Human laws relate to both impersonal and personal crimes. If I broke the 45 mph speed limit on my way to teach class, I would not feel I had violated any loving relationship. But suppose my wife, daughter, and I visited friends in Dallas who took us to Bennigan's for lunch, the Ports O'Call Restaurant for a Polynesian dinner, and Fair Park Auditorium Saturday night for a musical. Then Sunday afternoon they took us to Texas Stadium to watch the Cowboys play the Steelers. By this time we would really feel indebted for their many kindnesses. What if before we left, my wife hid silverware in her handbag, my daughter packed an electronic game, and I put three expensive commentaries in my briefcase. We would have broken a law, but more than that, we would have shown contemptuous disregard for the loving hospitality of our hosts.

So it is when we break the law of God. From our birth he has continually showered us with gifts. When we break his laws, we are violating a close, intense, warm, personal friendship. We are the scum of the earth. Who would do such things to a friend? Yet some of God's "friends" have very little compunction about violating his continually loving relationship. It is no surprise that he becomes so distraught over his ungrateful sons and daughters.

The Law Is God's

Yahweh gives his law out of love. He reveals guidelines to humans that they cannot discover on their own. Man does not earn the love of God by keeping his law. God gives his gifts and his love freely. Israel is told to keep the law so she will not be cut off from the gifts which God continually grants. The law does not stand apart from God. It is his. He does with it as he pleases. The law of God is not some abstract universal principle located in nature or beyond. The law is God's because he gave it. He gave it because he desires a faithful, continual, and regulated relationship with the works of his hands, especially man made in his image.

Sometimes people visualize the law of God as having a life of its own. It stands apart from both God and man for their scrutiny and interpretation. These people see God as bound by his law. Of course, God is faithful in promise. But he does with his law as he pleases and always to the benefit of humanity. Certain Israelites once came to Jerusalem to worship in the days of Hezekiah. They were from the north, and that kingdom had already fallen. They had a problem. They had not been in Jerusalem long enough to go through the regular cleansing ceremony. "Yet they ate the passover otherwise than as prescribed" (2 Chr. 30:18). They did so, however, without impunity, for Hezekiah prayed to the Lord on their behalf. "The LORD heard Hezekiah and healed the people" (2 Chr. 30:20).

When God desires, he can waive punishment for law-breaking. He can make decisions about his law as he goes along. Man is in no position to make those decisions for him. Man has no right to declare when God will or will not enforce his law. We have only the assignment to proclaim the ways of God. We have not been given the license to declare when God might waive the requirements.

The word "legalism" is not found in the Bible. However, if the word is used to describe an improper way of viewing the law from a biblical perspective, it might be a useful term. Legalism obviously brings to mind an unfavorable entity. Legalism is a mistaken position on how strictly the law must be observed. But from an Old Testament perspective, what is an overly strict interpretation? One "legalistic" position condemned in the Old Testament is the assumption that law is universal and impersonal and stands even prior to or superior to God himself. Instead, law in the Old Testament always refers to the loving rules provided by a merciful God. They do not inhere in the universe or stand apart from God. They are his. He issued them. Therefore, it is "legalistic" to talk about God's laws as if they are impersonal in the same manner as the laws of motion or the laws of gravity.

Sometimes, people disdainfully refer to others who see value in law as "legalists." In the Old Testament there is delight in, and respect and love for, the law of God. The Old Testament certainly does not denounce the law of God, only a mistaken understanding of it. For example, Amos decries sacrifices and tithes because people in his time thought they had fulfilled God's demands in that way. Amos made it clear that God demanded a total life which involved justice and righteousness (Amos 5:21-24). From an Old Testament perspective, the term "legalist" cannot refer to anyone who takes the law of God seriously. It can only apply to the person who has a mistaken perception of the law of God.

God's Love through His Law

Why were specific collections of Old Testament laws given? In searching out the reasons, we discover the hand of a loving, beneficent God. There are basically four collections of law in the Old Testament: (1) Exodus 20–40, (2) Leviticus, (3) Numbers 1–10 and (4) Deuteronomy.

1. **Exodus 20–40**. The covenant with the Ten Commandments in Exodus 20 is followed by a number of specific regulations for living in the land. The rest of the laws in Exodus pertain to the construction and furnishing of the tabernacle.

In the first section (chapters 20–23), it is clear that the basis for the law is the loving action of God. Yahweh's people are requested to behave in a certain manner because of the way Yahweh has behaved. In other words, like God, like people. Therefore, the laws are given so God's sons can be like him and enjoy his familial love. The sabbath rest is to be observed because God himself rested (Exod. 20:8-11). Israel is to treat strangers lovingly because, when they were strangers in Egypt, God treated them lovingly. "You shall not wrong or oppress a resident alien, for you were aliens in the land of Egypt" (Exod. 22:21). Because God has looked after the welfare of his people, they are to look after the welfare of others (Exod. 22:22-31).

In the New Testament, the expectations of God are much the same except that they grow out of the action of Christ. "As the Lord has forgiven you, so you also must forgive" (Col. 3:13). "Consider him who endured such hostility against himself from sinners, so that you may not grow weary or lose heart" (Heb. 12:3).

Yahweh gave detailed instructions for building the tabernacle so he could dwell among his people. What greater boon can we receive than that God, maker of heaven and earth, dwells in our midst? "And have them make me a sanctuary, so that I may dwell among them" (Exod. 25:8). (See also 25:21-22, which declares that God will appear above the mercy seat). When the tabernacle was completed, "The cloud covered the tent of meeting, and the glory of the LORD filled the tabernacle" (Exod. 40:34).

Out of his goodness God gave his people rules so he could dwell in their midst. Should a President decide to build a summer home in a specific location, the community would receive a list of rules pertaining to the security and privacy of the President's family. The people, however, probably would not see the rules as oppressive because they would consider it an honor for a President to vacation in their town. So the ancient people of God received the rules for the tabernacle as reflecting the beneficent concern of God. They were given so he could dwell in their midst. Christians likewise have such rules for the presence of Christ. "For where two or three are gathered in my name, I am there among them" (Matt. 18:20). The gathering must be in his name, and according to his ways.

2. Leviticus. The laws in Leviticus are basically concerned with the tabernacle, sacrifices, priests, dietary regulations, and feasts. Why did God give all these laws? Sometimes people read the food regulations and justify them on the basis of modern nutrition, disease, and hygiene. But Leviticus has its own reasons: "You shall be holy; for I the LORD your God am holy" (Lev. 19:1-2). God wants his people to be holy so he can be in close fellowship with them. "You shall be holy to me; for I the LORD am holy, and I have separated you from the other peoples to be mine" (Lev. 20:26).

The food regulations prevent humanity from eating what is foreign to the nature of God. The forbidden creatures were basically those which ate carrion (dead flesh), such as vultures and catfish. God is the living God. Death is opposite his nature. For that reason, anyone touching a corpse was required to go through a cleansing ceremony (Lev. 21:1-6).

> All creatures that swarm upon the earth are detestable; they shall not be eaten. Whatever moves on its belly, and whatever moves on all fours, or whatever has many feet, all the creatures that swarm upon the earth, you shall not eat; for they are detestable. You shall not make yourselves detestable with any creature that swarms; you shall

> not defile yourselves with them, and so become unclean. For I am the
> LORD your God; sanctify yourselves therefore, and be holy, for I am
> holy. You shall not defile yourselves with any swarming creature that
> moves on the earth (Lev. 11:41-44).

But what if the rules are violated? Because of the expectations of a Holy God, is there then no hope? Yahweh, a loving God, arranged it so that even an offender can be cleansed and made holy. The rules pertaining to sacrifice enabled God's people to be holy because through faith in God the blood of the sacrifice is the means through which sins are forgiven. "Whatever touches its flesh shall become holy" (Lev. 6:27). "Thus the priest shall make atonement on his behalf for his sin, and he shall be forgiven" (Lev. 4:26). God is life. God made creatures and injected his life in their blood. That blood in turn, purifies the sinner.

> For the life of the flesh is in the blood; and I have given it to you
> for making atonement for your lives on the altar; for, as life, it is the
> blood that makes atonement (Lev.17:11).

The laws in Leviticus are not arbitrary. They provide such perimeters so that the Israelites can be in fellowship with a holy God. Some say the blessings of the Old Testament are physical while those of the New Testament are spiritual. There is a seed of truth in this generalization since Abraham became wealthy but Peter did not. But what is meant by spiritual blessings if not close fellowship with God? God gave the regulations in Leviticus out of love to enable his people to walk daily with him. What can be more spiritual than a daily walk with God?

According to the Scriptures, God's laws are never arbitrary and without explanation. Baptism, for example, has a profound meaning. It shows our commitment to Jesus who died and arose (Rom. 6:1-12) and that we have been washed clean to be acceptable to a holy God (Titus 3:56). "Be perfect, therefore, as your heavenly Father is perfect" (Matt. 5:48).

3. Numbers 1–10. The early section of Numbers gives instructions for marching and for the role of the Levites. The rules are crucial because the welfare and victories of God's people depend on the presence of the tabernacle and the Levites. By their presence the people are kept from sinning and hence incurring the wrath of God. "But the Levites shall camp around the tabernacle of the covenant, that there may be no wrath on the congregation of the Israelites; and the Levites shall perform the guard duty of the tabernacle of the covenant" (Num. 1:53). And again in this case, the Levites serve the people, since, if violations do occur, the Levites offer sacrifices which bring about forgiveness. The sacrificial work of the Levites is efficacious, first, because they offer sacrifices for themselves (Lev. 8:12). Thus purified, they in turn offer sacrifices for the people.

> Moreover, I have given the Levites as a gift to Aaron and his sons from among the Israelites, to do the service for the Israelites at the tent of meeting, and to make atonement for the Israelites, in order that there may be no plague among the Israelites for coming too close to the sanctuary (Num. 8:19).

The rules for the Levites were for the welfare of the people. God's people therefore delight in his laws because God is good and his laws are for their benefit. People who keep the ways of God always benefit others around them. "For the unbelieving husband is made holy through his wife, and the unbelieving wife is made holy through her husband" (1 Cor. 7:14).

4. Deuteronomy. In Deuteronomy we learn that God gave the law so humans would know what to do in the land God gave them. If humans do what is proper, God will ward off the enemy and provide rain for the crops (7:12-16; 6:20-24; 11:8-17). Yahweh will furnish a productive land and a long life in the land. The laws are for man's good. "Then the LORD commanded us to observe all these statutes, to fear the

LORD our God, for our lasting good, so as to keep us alive, as is now the case" (Deut. 6:24).

> Hear therefore, O Israel, and observe them diligently, so that it may go well with you, and so that you may multiply greatly in a land flowing with milk and honey, as the LORD, the God of your ancestors, has promised you (Deut. 6:3).

In contrast, if the Israelites are not faithful to the law, they will lose all they received (Deut. 8:19-20). Failure to keep the law will result in a small harvest (28:15-19), disease and pestilence (28:25-27), and miscellaneous trouble (28:28-35). God gave his law out of love; without it his people perish rather than obtain the good life in his land. Even in the New Testament, God's rules enable man to live a longer and better life (Eph. 6:1-4).

Law for Other Nations

Other nations were also subject to the rules of God, though they did not receive law by special revelation as Israel did when Yahweh thundered at Sinai. Many of the prophets condemned other nations, showing that God held these nations subject to his ways. The grounds on which these nations were held accountable were not always obvious. In wisdom literature, all men were accountable to God because he built his ways into nature itself. They could therefore determine his ways by observing and learning from nature (Prov. 3:19,20; 8:22-36).

It may be that Amos had in mind these rules implanted in nature when he condemned the nations. He denounced Damascus for inhuman viciousness in war (1:3), Gaza for selling captives as slaves (1:6), Tyre for selling their brothers as slaves (1:9), Edom for harsh war techniques (1:11), the Ammonites for killing women with children (1:13), and the Moabites for burning the bones of the king of Edom (2:1). How did the nations know they did wrong? Apparently Amos believed that certain rights are universally obvious, much as presupposed by the United Nations Bill of Rights. But it is not clear whether Amos had in mind a natural law within nature or an inner law of the conscience. Nevertheless, if followed, these rules would improve the quality of man's life.

Christians live under rules growing out of Jesus Christ. The rules are specifically for people who have committed their lives to him. But other peoples are also subject to the ways of God who do not know him as Yahweh. "God will judge those outside" (1 Cor. 5:13). Therefore, the basic aim of Christians should be to bring people to Jesus Christ and encourage them to live by his rules (1 Cor. 5:12). But we must also make it clear to people who reject God that he likewise holds them accountable.

"The law of the LORD is perfect, reviving the soul; the decrees of the LORD are sure, making wise the simple; the precepts of the LORD are right, rejoicing the heart; the commandment of the LORD is clear, enlightening the eyes" (Psalm 19:7-8).

Yahweh loves forever. Even his laws divulge his inscrutable love.

Questions for Discussion

1. Are law and love opposites?

2. Show from the Old Testament that Yahweh's loving actions for his people always precede his giving of laws.

3. Is God's law impersonal?

4. Can humans earn the love and respect of God through keeping his law?

5. Is the law prior to God so that he himself is subject to it?

6. Are humans in a position to serve as referees for what God should do in respect to his law?

7. What is legalism as a pejorative activity from an Old Testament standpoint?

8. Why do the rules for constructing the tabernacle reflect God's love?

9. In what manner do the rules for sacrifice exemplify the love of God?

10. Are the blessings in the Old Testament material while those of the New Testament are spiritual?

11. How do the regulations regarding the Levites in Numbers show God's love?

12. Why is it in the Old Testament that nations other than Israel are subject to Yahweh's expectations?

8
Victory in the Conquest

Yahweh opened up the Red Sea and his people walked through. After such a momentous victory they lifted up his name, "The Lord is a warrior; the Lord is his name" (Exod. 15:3). Yahweh fought and won battles for his people, not because he relished blood and slaughter or continually sought vengeance, but for the sake of his name. Through people who know and respect him, Yahweh brings about his blessings (Exod. 15:13-18). He replaces people who contaminate and pollute his earth with people who inhabit it responsibly. The replacements may be far from perfect, but they are improvements over previous residents (Deut. 9:5).

From the Old Testament it is clear that God's efforts to woo and win humans to his way is more than simply a focus on individuals. God is concerned with nations. As the nation goes, so go most of the people in it. God therefore gets involved in the rise and fall of nations and in the migration of people. He fights for people who respect the rights of others. He defeats those who tread upon the weak and the poor and who ride roughshod across the globe defacing the earth. The

Old Testament constantly reminds us that God combats, struggles with, and persuades nations and groups of people as well as individuals. To counter the hordes of humans on earth, God leads forth his heavenly armies. He goes before them as commander. He is Lord Sabaoth, the Lord of Hosts. "Praise him, all his angels, praise him, all his host!" (Ps. 148:2).

The Way to Canaan

God loved his people. In the wilderness "the LORD went in front of them in a pillar of cloud by day, to lead them along the way, and in a pillar of fire by night, to give them light" (Exod. 13:21). The Lord always protects people who are his. He sees to it that the obstacles they face better equip them to serve him. They form the warehouse from which God distributes his good gifts to the other peoples of the earth. God remained with Israel all through the turbulent years in the wilderness. But he did not consign his people for wilderness living. Instead, he wanted them to sink their roots deeply into a land that would be their own. Not only did he consign the land, but he fought for and with them. He directed his heavenly hosts and his people on earth as would a general. "Do not fear them; for it is the LORD your God who fights for you" (Deut. 3:22). Many years earlier God had promised Abraham the land. Now the promise was about to be fulfilled. God loves to give gifts. He loves to give his people victory.

The first great victory of God's people in Canaan revealed that behind the earthly scene God's heavenly hosts are at work. The falling of the walls of Jericho was no natural phenomenon. It was the action of mighty heavenly armies. The story of Joshua, as he stood in the vicinity of Jericho on the day before the battle, makes this point. The victory over Jericho was a memorable battle against an ancient city. But actually it was no contest because the mighty armies of Yahweh assured the victory.

The story opens with Joshua contemplating battle. The city of Jericho is in the background (Josh. 5:13-15). Joshua seems to be in the mood of a football coach a day before the big game. As he paced about, he looked up and saw a man standing with a sword drawn in his hand. When Joshua asked whose side he was on, he said he was "commander of the army of the LORD" (Josh. 5:14). The man told Joshua to take off his shoes because the ground was holy. Various proposals have been made about this man's identity. But it seems best to conclude that it was Yahweh appearing in human form (Gen. 18).

The person described himself as "commander of the army of the LORD" (Josh 5:14). What does this mean? Yahweh describes himself as the "general of the armies." Several Scriptures tell how Yahweh gives victory to his people through the action of his heavenly armies. "With him were myriads of holy ones; at his right a host of his own" (Deut. 33:2). It is by the might of Yahweh's forces, not through overwhelming human armies and astute military strategy, that God's people win.

> Some take pride in chariots, and some in horses, but our pride is in the name of the LORD our God. They will collapse and fall, but we shall rise and stand upright. Give victory to the king, O LORD; answer us when we call (Ps. 20:7-9).

Yahweh Sabaoth at Jericho

The word "hosts" in Hebrew is *sabaoth*. It is a military term. In Joshua 5:14 the Hebrew word translated "army" ("commander of the army of the LORD") is *sabaoth*. In several prophets Yahweh Sabaoth is the standard designation of the God who commands the marauding, destroying armies.

So how can we understand the great victory at Jericho? Victory occurred because of the heavenly armies. The text affirms this. (1) God showed up at Jericho with his armies.

These hosts were not obvious to everyone. They were only seen through eyes of faith. (2) Human armies were involved, but for the rituals of marching and shouting, which were a show of faith. (3) Victory was assured when the heavenly hosts of Yahweh caused the walls to fall; then the human army entered to complete the victory. God works through his hosts behind the scenes to give his people victory. God's action fulfilled his earlier promise to Joshua (Deut. 31:23). Not only did he stand behind Joshua to give him encouragement, but he also helped fight. "You shall not fear them; for it is the LORD your God who fights for you" (Deut. 3:22).

Why did Jericho fall? The Old Testament tells us it was because of the heavenly hosts of Yahweh. For some modern interpreters, the story is simply ancient folklore, a neat miracle story from a credulous age. Others have tried to soften this obvious miracle by supplying natural explanations. At least two have been offered. *First*, it has been argued that at the exact time of the seventh shout an earthquake destroyed the walls. Earthquakes did occur in the regions (Amos 1:1), but this has no textual support. Even if God acted through an earthquake, it would still be an extraordinary act of God since the timing was so perfect. A *second*, perhaps more logical, suggestion is that the fall resulted from mud slides. The year reportedly was an unusually wet one. The ancient foundations of some city walls were dirt, not rock. Just as during the rainy season in California when homes on the canyon rims slide into the abyss, so the foundations slipped and the walls of Jericho came tumbling down. Of course, the vibrations from the tramping feet and the great shout were "the final straw that broke the camel's back."

Now even in the Old Testament God did work through natural channels. The winds drove in the quail to supply the meat for the wilderness wanderers (Num. 11:31). But the story of Joshua makes it perfectly clear that Jericho fell because of the presence of the heavenly hosts of Yahweh.

Yahweh Sabaoth and Warfare

In the Old Testament, victories and defeats depended on whose side Yahweh fought. He gave his people victory over the Egyptians and the occupants of the land of Canaan. In David's time, when the Philistines troubled the land, David claimed victory in the name of the Lord of hosts, not because of his own might. David said to the Philistine, Goliath, "You come to me with sword and spear and javelin; but I come to you in the name of the LORD of hosts, the God of the armies of Israel, whom you have defied" (1 Sam. 17:45).

David's statement makes it obvious that *Yahweh Sabaoth* is a military term. Notice how "LORD of hosts" is parallel to "God of the armies." The heavenly armies of Yahweh formed Israel's chief line of defense against enemies. Israel maintained a stable though perilous position among the nations through God's might and power.

But Yahweh only gave victory to his people when they showed their trust in him by faithfully following his laws. Prophets often wrote that Yahweh led enemy nations against Israel because the people had turned their backs on him. The enemy will destroy Jerusalem (Isa. 3:1). Because the people have "rejected the instruction of the LORD of hosts" (Isa. 5:24), Yahweh will signal for a nation afar off (5:26). As indicated by the imagery, that nation was obviously the powerful and destructive Assyria.

The people in Amos's time also turned their backs on God. As a result, Yahweh went over to the side of the enemy. Now he marched against his own people as Yahweh Sabaoth, general of the opposing armies. "Hear, and testify against the house of Jacob, says the Lord GOD, the God of hosts: On the day I punish Israel for its transgressions, I will punish the altars of Bethel, and the horns of the altar shall be cut off and fall to the ground" (Amos 3:13-14).

When Yahweh fought for his people, the army followed rules of warfare provided by Yahweh himself. Because these rules called for only token human participation, they clearly presupposed that the outcome depended on Yahweh and his heavenly hosts. God loved to give his people victory because through them he showered his blessings upon the nations. He continually worked to supplant people who polluted the earth through their inhumanity to man and animals. He replaced the incorrigible with those who searched for his ways and lived by his word.

Rules for Holy War

The most systematic presentation of the rules for holy war (war under the auspices of Yahweh) is found in Deuteronomy 20. First, there is an injunction not to be afraid since God himself is in the fray, and after all he prevailed over the Egyptians (20:1). Second, the priests, then the military commanders, addressed the troops. The order is important. In the twentieth century it would be preposterous to prepare for a great battle by beginning with an address from the chaplain. These addresses are usually made by the general, such as in the film version of Patton's march across Europe. In Deuteronomy 20, the priest supplies the encouragement, and the military officers identify the appropriate troops. Exempt are those who (1) have just built a house, (2) planted a vineyard, (3) recently acquired a wife, and (4) are fainthearted (20:5-9). If these rules applied today, there would be a rash of new houses and vineyards, weddings, and persons psychologically unprepared for war. Even in those days, the number of exempt persons totaled more than those who fought. How could successful warfare be carried on under such rules? Deuteronomy made it clear that victory belonged to Yahweh, not to superior human forces.

These rules conclude with the manner in which the conquered people and their land are to be treated. Two different rules pertain to the conquered people: (1) for people in cities far off (20:10-15) and (2) for those within the inherited land (20:16-18). Terms of peace are to be offered to cities on the way to the land. If, however, the city comes out to do battle, God's people will fight and God will give them victory (20:3-4). All the males are to be killed, but women, children, animals and material objects may be taken for spoil. The people of the far-off cities had a choice, and they were preserved or destroyed accordingly. However, all the people — even women and children — and animals in the land of Canaan were to be destroyed. "You must not let anything that breathes remain alive" (20:16).

The fact that Yahweh himself ordered the killing of women, babies, and pregnant mothers seems inhumanly cruel, and inexplicable if ordered by a loving God. But before we judge, we should listen to the reasons given in the text. These are to be destroyed "so that they may not teach you to do all the abhorrent things that they do for their gods, and you thus sin against the LORD your God" (Deut. 20:18).

The wickedness of these people was multiplied down through the centuries. Finally, it became so bad that God didn't know what else to do except obliterate them from the face of the earth. There was no point in sending in others as replacements since they would only be contaminated by such gross evil.

Nothing seems as cruel to us as the taking of a life. But according to the Scripture, what is ultimately important is not life itself, but the right way of life. A self-centered person who disrupts others and pollutes the earth is more harmful than someone who is dead. In fact, Scripture identifies such people as dead: "But the widow who lives for pleasure is dead even while she lives" (1 Tim. 5:6), and "they feast with you without fear, feeding themselves. . . . autumn trees without fruit, twice dead, uprooted" (Jude 12). A person faithful to God does not despair of losing life because God is the author of life and will give it anew (Phil. 1:21-26). The worse fear is a life of suffering for evil now and eternally. Jesus said, "Do not fear those who kill the body but cannot kill the soul; rather fear him who can destroy both soul and body in hell" (Matt. 10:28).

The Old Testament shows that God's plans for wiping out the Canaanites were long in the making. God is depicted as "not slow about his promise, as some think of slowness, but is patient with you, not wanting any to perish, but all to come to repentance" (2 Pet. 3:9). Indeed, he was "slow to anger," as he declared (Exod. 34:6).

You may have wondered why God did not provide Abraham the muscle to wipe out the Canaanites and take over the land immediately. You may have concluded that Abraham did not need all that real estate then, and that God had other assignments for his descendants in Egypt and only later did they need the whole land. But the text points to God's long forbearance. "And they shall come back here in the fourth generation; for the iniquity of the Amorites is not yet complete" (Gen. 15:16). God didn't base his decision to replace the Canaanites on a few minor infractions. He gave them at least five hundred years to get straightened around. But they went from bad to worse. God enabled the Israelites to replace them because his people stood head and shoulders above the Canaanites morally, not because Israel was without sin (Deut. 9:4-5).

What was so abominable about the Canaanites? Two items stand out: human and child sacrifice and cult prostitution.

> When you come into the land that the LORD your God is giving you, you must not learn to imitate the abhorrent practices of those nations. No one shall be found among you who makes a son or daughter pass through fire, or who practices divination, or is a soothsayer, or an augur, or a sorcerer, or one who casts spells, or who consults ghosts or spirits, or who seeks oracles from the dead. For whoever does these

> things is abhorrent to the LORD; it is because of such abhorrent prac-
> tices that the LORD your God is driving them out before you. You must
> remain completely loyal to the LORD your God. Although these nations
> that you are about to dispossess do give heed to soothsayers and
> diviners, as for you, the LORD your God does not permit you to do so
> (Deut. 18:9-14).

In regard to cult prostitution the people of Israel were charged to do the opposite of those who frequented the Baal shrines.

> None of the daughters of Israel shall be a temple prostitute; none
> of the sons of Israel shall be a temple prostitute. You shall not bring
> the fee of a prostitute or the wages of a male prostitute into the house
> of the LORD your God in payment for any vow, for both of these are
> abhorrent to the LORD your God (Deut. 23:17-18).

One of the claims for Baal was that he supplied fertility to people and animals. Therefore the sex act at the shrine was the way to appropriate his powers. Yahweh, however, does not achieve his ends through such acts. He gives fertility, but by his word. Therefore, this use of the sex act contradicts the ways of Yahweh.

So all these people were to be killed, and the slate wiped clean, because if women and children remained they would corrupt the standards of God's people. This happened when Solomon imported foreign wives (1 Kings 11:4-8).

Also, the rules for war say that trees producing nuts and fruit are not to be destroyed (Deut. 20:19). Warfare which indiscriminately destroys all vegetation is prohibited. Trees do not corrupt the earth. Man does.

Holy War Today

What implications do these rules have for modern war-fare? Christians sometimes cite the Old Testament as justifi-cation for involvement in war. If we fight under the autho-rization of the Old Testament, we should also fight under its rules. We should (1) give the chaplain a major role, (2) grant widespread exemptions, trusting that God will supply the victories, (3) fight wars of aggression only for the land God has promised us, and (4) preserve trees which supply food. Most countries commonly violate these rules in modern warfare.

Indeed Christians cannot justify war by the Old Testament because the land they have been promised is "the city of the living God, the heavenly Jerusalem" (Heb. 12:22). The territory the Christian is to take and protect is not geographical. It is the territory of the kingdom of God which transcends all national boundaries. The war cry of the Christian and his Lord is "the kingdom of God has come near; repent, and believe in the good news" (Mark 1:15).

Continuing Victories

After Israel occupied the land promised to Abraham and conquered by the armies under Joshua, the people were involved in mop-up and protection activities down through the centuries. Israel was most successful when the people trusted Yahweh and not their own might or diplomatic shrewdness. Yahweh was Lord of hosts both for and against his people, depending on their faithfulness.

During the days of the judges, God's people had their ups and downs depending on whether they lived by Yahweh's rules (Judg. 3:18-19). Once, after a long period of unfaithfulness and harassment by the Midianites, an angel appeared to Gideon at the hidden wine press where he was threshing wheat. The angel told Gideon he would deliver his people and assured him, "I will be with you, and you shall strike down the Midianites, every one of them" (Judg. 6:16).

As Gideon prepared for battle, God told him that he had too many people. He was therefore to select the men by the way they drank. Three hundred men remained after meeting God's criteria. Since 300 men were a drop in the bucket compared with the manifold hordes of the Midianites, Yahweh again proved that victory depended on his heavenly hosts. Through God's instructions, Gideon confused the Midianite camp by distributing men on every side. After dark the men of Gideon put up torches and blew trumpets. "When they blew the three hundred trumpets, the LORD set every man's sword against his fellow and against all the army" (Judg. 7:22).

Later, the prophets Elijah and Elisha served God and provided leadership to protect his people and their land. Their victories also were attributed to the presence of Yahweh and his heavenly hosts. At one time the Syrians were troubling Israel. The Syrian king, however, lost most of the battles because the Israelites always anticipated his strategy. He suspected that a traitor in his cabinet leaked secret information to Israelite leaders. When the king confided his suspicion to an advisor, he learned that the source of his trouble was Elisha. "It is Elisha, the prophet in Israel, who tells the king of Israel the words that you speak in your bedchamber" (2 Kgs. 6:12). Elisha became the object of the king's ire. "Go and find him where he is; I will send and seize him" (2 Kgs. 6:13). The king sent a whole army to take one man. When the servant of Elisha rose early the next morning, he was shocked to see the kings' horses and chariots. Elisha remained calm. He was convinced that one man and God form a majority. "Do not be afraid, for there are more with us than there are with them" (2 Kgs. 6:16). The servant no doubt thought that Elisha was out of his mind. But Elisha, full of confidence, prayed that the servant's eyes would be opened and behold, "the mountain was full of horses and chariots of fire all around Elisha" (2 Kgs. 6:17).

When Yahweh's man or woman is under attack, Yahweh appears with his mighty heavenly hosts. He is *Yahweh Sabaoth*. The forces of Yahweh work behind the scenes and can only be seen through the eyes of faith. "Are not all angels spirits in the divine service, sent to serve for the sake of those who are to inherit salvation" (Heb. 1:14)?

One phrase describing Elijah and Elisha underlined the fact that wherever they went, there the armies of Yahweh were also present. When Elijah was about to die, he was taken up into heaven by a chariot of fire and horses of fire. As Elisha watched he cried out, "Father, father! The chariots of Israel and its horsemen!" (2 Kgs. 2:12). This exclamation obviously referred to the manner in which Elijah was taken into heaven. But it also pointed out that wherever this man of God appeared, the hosts of Yahweh were also present. Israel didn't require mighty earthly armies when Elijah showed up. The same phrase was used of Elisha at his death (2 Kgs. 13:14), indicating that victory was assured when he appeared at the battle camp.

Prophets chided God's people for trusting their own might and diplomatic expertise rather than Yahweh Sabaoth. When Sargon II of Assyria died in 705 B.C., Judah rebelled. The king of Judah looked upon its situation as precarious and sent an ambassador to Egypt. Egypt became a ready ally, promising horsemen and chariots. But Isaiah considered all these efforts as wasted motion. God's people needed to trust Yahweh. He could supply heavenly armies to protect his people.

> Alas for those who go down to Egypt for help and who rely on hors-es, who trust in chariots because they are many and in horsemen because they are very strong, but do not look to the Holy One of Israel or consult the LORD! (Isa. 31:1).

Victory for Israel will come from the Lord of Hosts. "So the LORD of hosts will come down to fight upon Mount Zion and upon its hill. Like birds hovering overhead, so the LORD of hosts will protect Jerusalem; he will protect and deliver it, he will spare and rescue it" (Isa. 31:4-5).

The love of God is steadfast. He will always send his heavenly armies to fight for his faithful ones. One faithful believer and Yahweh make a majority, whatever the circumstances.

Questions for Discussion

1. Why does God involve himself in justice in and among the nations?

2. What does *Yahweh Sabaoth* mean? What are the implications?

3. Did Yahweh ever lead his hosts against his own people? Why?

4. How do the rules for war in Deuteronomy 20 indicate that faith in Yahweh is the deciding factor?

5. According to Deuteronomy, why did God order the Canaanites destroyed? Did they deserve it?

6. Why were the nut and fruit trees to be preserved?

7. Can modern Christians justify war based on what they find in the Old Testament?

8. How did Gideon win a major battle against the Midianites?

9. Why were Elijah and Elisha identified as "the chariots of Israel and its horsemen?"

10. Do one person and Yahweh make a majority?

11. Should Christians support the buildup of military prowess?

12. How should modern believers protect themselves against their enemies?

9
Inheritance of the Land

And because he loved your ancestors, he chose their descendants after them. He brought you out of Egypt with his own presence, by his great power, driving out before you nations greater and mightier than yourselves, to bring you in, giving you their land for a possession, as it is still today (Deut. 4:37-38).

God's gift of land illustrates his undying love. In the text above, we learn that God's actions from Egypt to Palestine resulted from his great love for his people. Then he also gave them land as an inheritance because he loved them. God's heart reached out to his people who were homeless, and because he loved them he gave them a land.

A farmer in Iowa owned 640 acres of rich farmland. He and his wife were getting on in years. A young man came to work for them. He later married, had children, and felt the responsibilities for a growing family. He had worked for the farmer about ten years when the needs of his family commenced to exceed his income. He and his wife became acutely concerned about their future. It seemed to them that they needed to buy a farm of their own in order to meet the anticipated needs both of themselves and their children. When the farm owner and his wife became aware of their concerns, they too gave serious thought to the situation. They liked the young couple very much, and they were reluctant to once again seek for new help. They had almost come to love the employee and his wife like a son and daughter-in-law. They understood the predicament. They thereupon decided to give the couple a percentage of the farm earnings and in their will upon their death, leave the farm to them. The young couple received the unexpected, but magnificent gift with gladness and the future of all concerned was secured.

Yahweh also understood the predicament of his son. In the ancient world, a plot of ground was crucial if a family was to sustain themselves. Almost everyone had at least a small parcel upon which to grow beans, squash, and other vegetables. So God gave his people land so they could anticipate a secure future. Humans are future oriented. They are always making plans for the future. People are always anxious about how their future will turn out. Much effort is expended upon securing the future in respect to position and job. God encourages this trait. He himself has made promises about the future of humanity and has requested trust in his willingness and ability to make it turn out as he has said.

Yahweh is future oriented. "I will be what I will be" (Exod. 3:14). And God is well aware that humans must sustain themselves from day to day in order to be free for grander deeds. The affirmation that "one does not live by bread alone" (Deut. 8:3) recognizes that bread is necessary if man is to live. Man, however, needs more than bread (for example, daily fellowship with God), but he has to have bread in order to live.

For 600 years the homeless descendants of Abraham wandered on earth. But they lived in anticipation because of God's promise: "I am the LORD who brought you from Ur of the Chaldeans, to give you this land to possess" (Gen. 15:7).

They were not given the land so they could be rich and become self-indulgent. God intended for them to be affluent, but he wanted them to use their wealth for the good of others. Servanthood was the object of the legacy he bestowed (Ps. 136:21-22).

Yahweh loved his people, and he gave them a land. He gave it without asking questions, but it was not a "no strings attached" situation. He gave it under the supposition that as they freely received they would freely give (Matt. 10:8). "We love because he first loved us" (1 John 4:19). They were to concern themselves with the fatherless and widows in the land because they knew what it was like to be without land in the desert. They had received the land as a gift. In turn, they were to distribute the produce of the land to others as gifts (Deut. 24:17-22).

This chapter will examine land under three topics: (1) the inheritance as a gift, (2) the proper attitude toward and use of the inheritance, and (3) circumstances under which Israel will be disinherited, or lose the land.

The Inheritance as a Gift

The Old Testament illustration of God's people inheriting a land comes from the customs of the time. It portrays in a profound sense the means through which Israel came to possess Palestine. The analogy is not totally consistent, but analogies are seldom appropriate for consistent and rigorous application. Despite some haze, the message shines through strong and clear. Israel did not earn Palestine through its own efforts. Israel did not inherit the land as a natural child. The people received it as a loving gift from Yahweh.

The love of God for Israel was like that of the Iowa farmer mentioned earlier. The hired man was not a son. There was no way he could earn a farm worth almost a million dollars. He received it because of the grace and love of the owner, not because of who he was. Likewise, Israel is depicted as an adopted son of Yahweh. "A wandering Aramean was my ancestor; he went down into Egypt and lived there as an alien, few in number, and there he became a great nation, mighty and populous" (Deut. 26:5).

Ezekiel's analogy is that of a bride rather than a son, but the same thesis is obvious (Ezek. 16:3-4,8). Israel was taken as a bride, but not as a daughter from a respected family. Israel was an unwanted, exposed child. The ancient world had no children's homes or foster child care as we have now. An unwanted child was exposed to the elements — in Greece on a mountainside, in arid regions in an open field (Ezek. 16:5). Israel, therefore did not have the rights of a natural daughter.

In Hosea's analogy, Israel was a wayward son adopted by Yahweh as a child in Egypt (Hos. 11:1). God brought him home to Palestine to raise him and prepare him to take over his estate. In a discouraging moment after reflecting on the son's ingratitude, God determined to take him back to Egypt (that is, back to the children's home). But he soon was over-powered by divine love and could not (Hos. 11:8-9).

Unlike Aeneas of ancient Rome, Israel was an adopted son of God. Like other ancient kings, Aeneas had a human and a divine parent and thus received kingship by divine right. His mother was the goddess of love, Aphrodite. Israel had no divine right to the land of Palestine. The Old Testament makes no claims for anyone being of divine descent. Kings might be referred to as sons of Yahweh — "You are my son" (Ps. 2:7) — but not because they literally descended from Yahweh. Their human parents were clearly evident. They were adopted "sons of Yahweh." Israel had no natural claim on the land of Palestine. Israel also did not deserve it through centuries of hard labor for Yahweh the landlord. Israel received the land because God was a God of grace, one whose steadfast love never ceases.

Unlike today, most adoptions in the ancient world were of adults not children, and by a person of some wealth and without any heirs. Today a couple without children might leave their estate to an institution. Ancient couples with no children adopted adult males whose lives pleased them, and made them heirs of the estate. At one time, in despair of ever having children of their own, Abraham and Sarah went that route (Gen. 15:2). "But Abram said . . . 'I continue childless, and the heir of my house is Eliezer of Damascus? . . . You have given me no offspring, and so a slave born in my house is to be my heir.'"

Pursuing the analogy of adoption, we see that Yahweh, childless on earth, adopted Abraham and left his estate to him. The descendants of Abraham then became proud possessors of Yahweh's magnificent gift.

Yahweh owned the whole earth, not just Palestine.

> For every wild animal of the forest is mine, the cattle on a thousand hills. I know all the birds of the air, and all that moves in the field is mine. If I were hungry, I would not tell you, for the world and all that is in it is mine (Ps. 50:10-12).

Yahweh owned everything because he created it (Ps. 115:15). He gave of his possessions to all peoples, not just to Israel (Ps. 115:16). But he reserved a special place for Israel. As Yahweh's adopted son, Israel received the special territory which Yahweh had reserved for himself (Deut. 32:8-9). The Masoretic Hebrew in 32:8 reads "sons of Israel" rather than "sons of God." However, the more likely meaning is, as translated in the NRSV, that Yahweh fixed the number of earthly nations according to the number of his heavenly sons (see also Job 1:6). But Israel was a special son, and therefore received a special inheritance, that is, the land of Israel. Of the nations Israel alone is an adopted son of Yahweh. Israel's inheritance is a special gift from a gracious, eternally loving God.

The land was a gift because not only did God play a major role in the conquest of the land, Israel received it, not as undeveloped territory, but with all the improvements.

> When the LORD your God has brought you into the land that he swore to your ancestors, to Abraham, to Isaac, and to Jacob, to give you — a land with fine, large cities that you did not build, houses filled with all sorts of goods that you did not fill, hewn cisterns that you did not hew, vineyards and olive groves that you did not plant . . . . (Deut. 6:10-11).

Furthermore, the waters to replenish the grass and the produce came not by human effort, but from Yahweh himself.

> For the land that you are about to enter to occupy is not like the land of Egypt, from which you have come, where you sow your seed and irrigate by foot like a vegetable garden. But the land that you are crossing over to occupy is a land of hills and valleys, watered by rain from the sky (Deut. 11:10-11).

Living in the Land

When Israel finally received the land, how were they as a people to live in it? First, the proper response was gratitude because of God's gracious gift. Second, the land did not actually belong to Israel; Yahweh retained the title. But Yahweh wanted his children to sustain themselves. He didn't want them to be homeless. The Israelites often assumed that they had to make their own way in the world and that they could live as they pleased. But Yahweh's adopted son had no special claim on his land. God gave him the rights to it so he would in turn share it with others. If he did not use it as God intended, then God asserted that he would reclaim it.

God's ultimate ownership of the land is obviously set forth in the Old Testament rules concerning the land. The principles behind these rules are important for Christians today. Christians must look out for the welfare of others so that they are able to sustain themselves (Acts 6:1; Gal. 2:10; 6:10).

Once the land was distributed, it remained in the possession of the same tribal unit forever (Lev. 25:23-24). If the land happened to pass into the hands of new owners, the law provided the channels through which it would ultimately return to the original owner (Lev. 25:25-28). The land was not to be used for wheeling and dealing. God distributed it equitably among his people so that each could grow food and sustain himself. It was especially important in the ancient world for a person to own a small plot of land. Without land people were forced to depend on charity or sell themselves as slaves. Therefore, a person who obtained the property of another deprived him of his livelihood. And since ultimate ownership is Yahweh's, the person who wheels and deals in land flaunts God's ownership of the earth.

Ahab's acquisition of Naboth's vineyard tested the property law. Naboth lived in critical times. Ancient paths were being ignored because Ahab the king had married Jezebel, the daughter of the king of the Sidonians — that is, a Phoenician. Because of Jezebel, Ahab built a house and an altar for Baal in Samaria (1 Kgs. 16:32). During this period of disregard for the laws of Yahweh, Ahab coveted Naboth's vineyard (1 Kgs. 21:14). Naboth refused to sell, but not simply because he attached sentimental value to the piece of property. He refused because of the law of God. "Do not remove the ancient landmark that your ancestors set up" (Prov. 22:28). The prophets railed against people like Ahab who flouted the property laws (Isa. 5:8; Mic. 2:1-2). Jezebel, however, had no compunction about disobeying the ways of Yahweh. So by a ruse she arranged Naboth's death, and Ahab soon went out to possess the vineyard. Meanwhile Yahweh told Elijah to meet Ahab at the vineyard and denounce him to his face because of his open contempt for the law of God (1 Kgs. 21:20).

What important points do these land rules make? First, whatever man possesses he has received as a gift from God. "Every generous act of giving, with every perfect gift, is from above, coming down from the Father of lights" (Jas. 1:17). The Levitical law, of course, guarantees property, but the owner knows God is the real proprietor. The Old Testament view of land is neither communistic nor socialistic, because land is not held in common by all people or controlled by the state. But neither is it a free enterprise which denies ultimate proprietorship to God. If by free enterprise we mean the freedom to exploit God's resources as we please like Ahab did, we have no justification in the Scriptures. Leviticus says each person should be free to use the resources God has provided to sustain himself. If he has more than he needs, he should open the doors of his warehouse to the poor, and to the widows and orphans.

Second, when a person has enough for his own needs, he does not seek to acquire more. The more possessions owned by a few, the less each individual participates in the good gifts of God. Jesus criticized people whose goal in life was to build bigger barns (Luke 12:13-21) rather than be sensitive to the needs of God's creatures (Luke 12:32-34). In countries today where land is owned only by a few or owned by the state and controlled by a few, poverty is widespread and many people suffer.

What right do people have to acquire more than they need and live luxuriously while depriving others of a suitable livelihood? They did not create the land. God made the heavens and the earth. In the eyes of God, they have no more right to God's real estate than anyone else, especially God's faithful servants. Therefore, God's person lives so that all of God's creatures may equitably enjoy his good gifts.

Third, as already noted, a person who has been fortunate enough to receive from God more than he needs should share it with others who are less fortunate. God planned for his people to be blessed and in turn bless others around them. Israel was once a slave and a stranger in a foreign land, but God gave the people land and resources. Israel's proper response was thus to share with strangers and unfortunate people (Exod. 22:21-24). According to Jesus, God gives us gifts so that we may give to others. The more we give others, the more we receive from him to give. "Give, and it will be given to you. A good measure, pressed down, shaken together, running over, will be put into your lap; for the measure you give will be the measure you get back" (Luke 6:38).

Deuteronomy set out specific ways to help the needy. It was not so much by doling out goods but by helping people help themselves. You help a child by tying his shoes, but you can help him more by teaching him to tie them himself. The olive trees, vineyards, and fields were not to be stripped bare so that the widows, orphans, and poor people could follow the reapers and glean enough to sustain themselves (Deut. 24:19-22). A person who realizes he has benefited abundantly from the grace of God is concerned about the equitable distribution of God's gifts to meet human needs. She doesn't simply pass out money. She works creatively to help needy people sustain themselves through their own efforts.

God gave land so his people would not be without. He loves to give. In turn, he expects his people to take after him. "Like father, like son!" The prophets declared that a compassionate concern for the needy is at the heart of Old Testament faith. Isaiah complained about the sinfulness of Israel. Although they did not forsake the temple or fail to sacrifice, they ignored justice and equity for the fatherless and the widows (Isa. 1:23). They needed to "learn to do good; seek justice, rescue the oppressed, defend the orphan, plead for the widow" (Isa. 1:17). Amos said almost nothing about idolatry, but he talked plenty about injustice toward the poor. "Hear this, you that trample on the needy, and bring to ruin the poor of the land" (Amos 8:4-6). Amos predicted that because

God's people used the gifts of God to their own selfish ends, they would lose what they possessed (Amos 6:4-7).

Disinheritance

Israel's failure to live according to the ways of God indicated ingratitude for his loving gifts. As we saw in the wilderness section, Yahweh put obstacles in the path of his sons to bring them to their senses in hopes they would return to him. If God's sons persist in their willfulness and self indulgence, he continues the punishment. If nothing works, he finally disinherits them by taking away the land. "I will strike them with pestilence and disinherit them" (Num. 14:12; cf. 2 Kgs. 21:14-15).

How were God's people to understand the loss of their land which God lovingly supplied? How could he provide roots and security, then take them away? In 721 B.C., Sargon II, king of Assyria, marched westward into Israel and destroyed Samaria, its capital. Almost 150 years later (587 B.C.) Jerusalem fell to the Babylonians under Nebuchadnezzar. People in both lands, especially Jerusalem, thought that since Yahweh gave the land, the capital city was impregnable. In fact, under Hezekiah in 701 B.C., the city miraculously survived the onslaught of Sennacherib the Assyrian. Because of that escape, people ridiculed Jeremiah when he charged that the city would fall if God's people didn't change their ways. The temple of Yahweh was in the midst of the city. He himself appeared above the mercy seat. Since God resided in the city, it was impervious to attack. But Jeremiah asserted that their confidence was baseless (Jer. 7:3-4). Yahweh could always withdraw and leave the city defenseless. Jeremiah and the other prophets were certain that God would disinherit his people and they would lose the land by willfully ignoring his rule that life is to be lived by helping others.

Many centuries earlier Moses told the people that once they were in the land and doing well, they would be tempted to think they earned what they had. If this happened, they would be in trouble. If they turned their backs on God, they would lose the land God gave them (Deut. 8:17-19). So according to the historians, the reasons for Israel's ups and downs was their waywardness, their indifference to the poor, and ingratitude for God's gracious gifts. This is clear in the historical analysis of the fall of Samaria (2 Kgs. 17:7-18).

Because of misuse of God's gifts Christians today may also lose their inheritance. The kingdom of God can fall into the hands of others (Rom. 11:20-24). Just because we rally around the name of Christ and his church, we are not impregnable. We are impregnable only if we do the will of God (Matt. 7:21-23). His will is that we "bear one another's burdens, and in this way . . . fulfill the law of Christ" (Gal. 6:2).

But God will not deprive his people forever. He will always save a remnant of the faithful to reoccupy the land. "I will restore the fortunes of my people Israel, and they shall rebuild the ruined cities and inhabit them" (Amos 9:13-15). God always opens his heart for his faithful ones, however few they may be. God loves forever. He loves to give his people the security of land. In turn, he expects them to enhance the security of others.

Questions for Discussion

1. Why was land so important in ancient Israel?

2. Why did Yahweh promise the land to Abraham and then give it centuries later?

3. How did Yahweh expect his people to use the land?

4. Did Israel deserve their land by birth or natural rights?

5. In what way does the land continue to be Yahweh's gift to Israel?

6. Why was it wrong to buy and sell land in Israel?

7. What is the point of the story about Naboth's vineyard?

8. Does Leviticus favor a free enterprise outlook on land ownership?

9. How may God's people live so as to enable all of God's creatures to equitably share in his good gifts?

10. What is God's ultimate solution for those who fail to be concerned about the needy?

11. Will God's people ultimately disappear from the face of the earth as the result of unfaithfulness?

12. How does God's gift of the land show his constant love for Israel? Does God involve himself more in permanent resources for sustenance than in fielding spur-of-the-moment requests?

10
A Shepherd for His People

He chose his servant David, and took him from the sheep-
folds; from tending the nursing ewes he brought him to be
the shepherd of his people Jacob, of Israel, his inheritance.
With upright heart he tended them, and guided them with
skillful hand (Ps. 78:70-72).

God has always loved women and men who respond
to his overtures. The Old Testament singles out
David as special among the numerous Godfearers.
Why did God choose David? The writer of Psalms
says God chose him to be "the shepherd of his people Jacob,
of Israel, his inheritance."

God reveals his plans in his promises. He promised
Noah he would never again destroy the earth by flood. He
promised Abraham that through him and his seed, he would
continue his good gifts to humankind. The seed of Abraham
would become a mighty nation and be a light to other
nations. Through that nation Yahweh would continue his
work of blessing man made in his image.

But God's nation had problems. It was harassed by enemies. Sometimes it ignored the ways of God. It tended to lack

He Loves Forever A Shepherd for His People

strong pro-Yahweh leadership. So God chose David to further his loving concerns. He chose David as a shepherd of his people to lead them in his paths. The promise to David had far-reaching ramifications. In that promise Yahweh announced a line of leadership that would be forever. How is that possible? Few nations have had one line of leaders for more than 500 years. So how could God promise David that his seed would reign forever?

The Call of David

Let's look at the events which led to the choosing of David. About 1200 B.C., 700 years after Abraham's death, God's people settled in the gift land after the early conquests. But even at Joshua's death, pockets of Jebusites, Philistines and others remained. For the next 200 years God raised up leaders for specific tasks. They were later known as judges — Deborah, Samson, and Samuel, among others. Yahweh worked powerfully through these people, but continuity was missing.

Late in the eleventh century winds of change stirred in the air. Under Samuel the armies managed to retake certain cities from the Philistines, and there was peace with the Amorites (1 Sam. 7:14). But Samuel was getting old, and his sons didn't seem like prime prospects for taking over his judgeship because, like Eli's sons, they "took bribes and perverted justice." The Philistines threatened once again. To many leaders, it seemed to be an appropriate moment to appoint a king like other nations. Israel had not yet gone that route. Israel did not need a king — Yahweh himself was king. When the leaders tried to make Gideon king after his brilliant successes against the Midianites, he responded, "I will not rule over you, and my son will not rule over you; the LORD will rule over you" (Judg. 8:23). But now Samuel was old, and the leaders thought the time was ripe (1 Sam. 8:45). Samuel was highly displeased. No doubt he considered the demand a reflection on his life's work. But Yahweh told Samuel to comply with the people's request, so Samuel anointed Saul of the tribe of Benjamin as king of Israel (1 Sam. 10:1). Saul thus became God's anointed (Hebrew, *mashiach*), a title which would have great future significance.

Saul reigned for about twenty years, but early in his reign he displeased the Lord by bringing home spoil from a foray into Amalek (1 Sam. 15:10). Saul's excuse was that he brought the animals back to make a sacrifice to God in Gilgal. Samuel then made a point which rang throughout Israel's history and even into our own. "Surely, to obey is better than sacrifice, and to heed than the fat of rams" (1 Sam. 15:22).

Did God make a mistake in choosing Saul? Yes and no. Saul did not turn out as God hoped. In that sense, it was a mistake. But even here the love of God is obvious. God has high hopes for every creature made in his image. He especially wants them to become great leaders — shepherds of his people. Sometimes God's hopes are dashed when prospective leaders refuse to obey. God longs for and encourages obedience, but he does not force it. Saul turned out to be a false shepherd.

Samuel thereupon was charged with anointing a new king. The successor was David, youngest son of Jesse. David was experienced in classic shepherding. He had spent his days herding his father's sheep (1 Sam. 16:11).

It was a few years before David succeeded to the kingship. Saul saw him as a personal threat and sought his life. David gathered a band of guerrilla fighters and lived among the Philistines. Finally, Saul was wounded in battle and killed himself (1 Sam. 31:1-6). David went to dwell in Hebron, and there the men of Judah anointed him king (2 Sam. 2:4). After later victories over the sons of Saul, the elders of Israel came to Hebron and also anointed David their king (2 Sam. 5:3). David was now declared king over all Israel.

The Great King

David was a great king, a man after God's own heart (1 Sam. 13:14). He was an outstanding warrior and an impressive ruler. He established the borders of a mighty empire stretching from the River of Egypt to the Euphrates River. He was a man of many talents, many moods and many weaknesses. Not only was he a great political leader in establishing his Jerusalem capital, he was a committed religious leader. He brought the tabernacle to Jerusalem, then the ark of the Lord. He instituted a worship leader's rotation. He encouraged the writing of psalms and even wrote several himself. But above all, he was a true shepherd to the people of God. He led them in worship of Yahweh. Because of his efforts, his nation was blessed, and in turn Israel was a blessing to its neighbors. David brought peace to his region. Throughout his life he trusted and obeyed the Lord.

Of course, David sinned. But when he sinned, he repented and changed his ways. He even led his people in repentance. David's son Solomon later commenced his kingship with an impressive singular commitment to Yahweh. But as he grew older, he was influenced by his many wives, the daughters of neighboring kings. He soon exhibited a divided loyalty for he also took up worship of their gods.

> King Solomon loved many foreign women along with the daughter of Pharaoh: Moabite, Ammonite, Edomite, Sidonian, and Hittite women, from the nations concerning which the LORD had said to the Israelites, "You shall not enter into marriage with them, neither shall they with you; for they will surely incline your heart to follow their gods"; Solomon clung to these in love. Among his wives were seven hundred princesses and three hundred concubines; and his wives turned away his heart. For when Solomon was old, his wives turned away his heart after other gods; and his heart was not true to the LORD his God, as was the heart of his father David (1 Kgs. 11:1-4).

As far as we know Solomon never committed adultery, then tried to cover it up by murdering the husband, as did David. But David had an undivided heart. He worshiped Yahweh his God and him alone he served. It was for that reason that he was a man after God's own heart, not Solomon.

Hebrew historians and interpreters later weighed and sifted the reigns of David's successors by the standards of David's faithfulness and commitment. It was written of Hezekiah: "He did what was right in the sight of the LORD, just as his ancestor David had done" (2 Kgs. 18:3). Jereboam I, however, failed to measure up to the standards of David. "You have not been like my servant David, who kept my commandments and followed me with all his heart" (1 Kgs. 14:8).

Toward the end of David's reign God made an impressive promise to David because of his love for him. The promise was a blessing for David and all his descendants forever. All the nations would benefit too. In Judah's later history, the promise to David provided stability in the midst of uncertainty, hope when times were hopeless, and permanence in times of change. Even in dark days when the countryside had been ravaged and Jerusalem destroyed, the promise to David provided a ray of hope.

Psalm 89 gives us the most vivid expression of the promise or covenant with David.

> Forever I will keep my steadfast love for him, and my covenant with him will stand firm. I will establish his line forever, and his throne as long as the heavens endure. If his children forsake my law and do not walk according to my ordinances, if they violate my statutes and do not keep my commandments, then I will punish their transgression with the rod and their iniquity with scourges; but I will not remove from him my steadfast love, or be false to my faithfulness (Ps. 89:28-33).

Yahweh did indeed love David and his seed forever. He did not put up with iniquity of individual kings. They were judged according to the laws of Moses. But the descendants of David always will be Yahweh's kings. They will shepherd his people forever.

Concrete Fulfillment of the Promise

God's promises deal with the real lives of men. According to the Old Testament, God worked with specific men and women right where they lived. He didn't work several feet above the earth, and he wasn't isolated in heavenly regions. We can trace in the Old Testament the way Yahweh kept his promise to David. But the promises of Yahweh sometimes take surprising twists. We may think we can predict how he will keep his word. But he keeps it his own way, not ours. He is faithful in promise. He loves forever. At the same time, he will be who he will be. He will act for his reasons and according to his purposes.

Why did the kingdom of Israel divide, leaving David's descendant Rehoboam ruling a small segment on the southern end of the land? We are familiar with the answer that greedy Rehoboam took the advice of the young men and increased taxation, and the opportunist and idolater Jereboam capitalized on the discontent and engineered a successful rebellion in the north (1 Kgs. 12). But 1 Kings 11 answers this question from the perspective of the promise of God to David.

The turnabout in Solomon's commitment to Yahweh triggered the division. Yahweh told David that if his sons violated his statutes he would "punish their transgression with the rod and their iniquity with scourges" (Ps. 89:32). The sons of David had it made. Yahweh loved them and committed his caring acts for them even before they were born. They didn't have to do anything to secure or merit that love. But when they turned away from Yahweh, he turned away from them and withdrew his love.

Solomon lost God's love through a divided heart. "For when Solomon was old, his wives turned away his heart after other gods" (1 Kgs. 11:4). Solomon violated the first commandment in the Mosaic covenant: "You shall have no other gods before me" (Exod. 20:3). God didn't decide to punish Solomon immediately. "The LORD, the LORD, a God merciful and gracious, slow to anger" (Exod. 34:6). Yahweh "had appeared to him twice, and had commanded him concerning this matter, that he should not follow other gods; but he did not observe what the LORD commanded" (1 Kgs. 11:9-10).

So God had a decision to make. How should he punish Solomon? He could bring in violent armies from the east as he did later. In this case, however, he opted for an internal division. He tore away a large chunk of Solomon's kingdom and gave it to Jereboam. What a high price Solomon paid — a price that was to be exacted century after century! But then Solomon turned his back on David's long suit, a daily walk with God. Yahweh desires communion, fellowship, steadfast love with and from man. He desires these traits because they are also his own.

Yahweh was so angered that perhaps he wanted to end the dynasty of David right then. But he had made a promise. "I will not, however, tear away the entire kingdom; I will give one tribe to your son, for the sake of my servant David and for the sake of Jerusalem, which I have chosen." (1 Kgs. 11:13). Here we see how God carried out the details of his promise to David. This illustrates both parts of the covenant. The promise to maintain the dynasty of David was upheld forever. The promise of punishment for unfaithfulness was also exacted. We probably would not have expected the punishment to be the loss of a large part of the kingdom. But our ways are not necessarily God's. He will be who he will be. Our own limited thoughts seldom anticipate the outer limits of God's action. We should be suspicious of persons who are eager to assert what God will or will not do.

Yahweh always looks for leaders to work through. He raises up persons to lead and shepherd his people. But sometimes God's shepherds become neglectful. They quit watching the flock. Then they get wrapped up in self-interests and quit walking with God. God is hurt. He tries to get them back on track. But if nothing changes, he determines punishments which may affect God's people for many generations. "Do not presume to say to yourselves, 'We have Abraham as our ancestor'; for I tell you, God is able from these stones to raise up children to Abraham. Even now the ax is lying at the root of the trees; every tree therefore that does not bear good fruit is cut down and thrown into the fire" (Matt. 3:9-10).

Did God Keep His Promise to David?

David commenced his reign about 1000 B.C. From that time until 587 B.C., or 413 years later, David's descendants reigned in Jerusalem. Four hundred years is a long time. English-speaking people made their first permanent settlement in America at Jamestown, Virginia, May 14, 1607, less than 400 years ago. Very few of the numerous Egyptian dynasties lasted more than 200 years and possibly none longer than 300. The dynasties of the northern kingdom were all relatively short. The longest was that of Jehu (842–746 B.C.), just less than 100 years.

So David's dynasty was amazingly long. Despite the lengthy succession, however, the dynasty came to a screeching halt when the Babylonians destroyed Jerusalem. We could extend the dynasty beyond 587. Jehoiachin at eighteen was defeated by the Babylonians in 597 and taken to Babylon. He was replaced by Zedekiah, but to many, Zedekiah was only a provisional ruler. Jehoiachin (Jeconiah) had seven sons (1 Chr. 3:17-18), and an effort to restore the kingship to David's descendants occurred about 515 B.C.

with Jehoiachin's grandson Zerubbabel (Hag. 2:21-22). The rule of David's descendants obviously ended there.

In the New Testament period 500 years later the Herodians ruled. The first of the Herods, Herod the Great (40–4 B.C.), was of Idumean or Edomite origin, though he considered himself a Jew and was so regarded by his contemporaries. The radicals of the period considered the kingship of the Herods invalid based on the promise to David. We must therefore ask if Yahweh broke his promise. Later Old Testament writings make it clear that expectancy of rule by David's descendants remained despite the long lapse. A long lapse was not precluded by the promise. The author of Kings says that Manasseh was so wicked that Yahweh simply permitted the kingship to dissolve (2 Kgs. 21:10-15).

Yahweh will be who he will be. He will interpret his covenant in his own way. In some future time God was to reestablish rule by David's seed. The incredibly good news of the first disciples of Jesus was that God had kept his promise in an unexpected way. They affirmed that Jesus, Son of God and descendant of David through Mary, now reigned over the kingdom of God. This new kingdom reached into all the nations. It knew no boundaries. It would eventually traverse both the earth and eternity. Acts 2 argues that Jesus is a descendant of David and now reigns at the right hand of God. He is the fulfillment of the promise "I will establish his line forever" (Acts 2:33-36; Ps. 89:29; Matt. 1:1; 12:23). God did not forget his promise! Jesus, son of David, reigns. His reign will be forever. He will not succumb to the iniquities of the other descendants of David and be deposed. He "in every respect has been tested as we are, yet without sin" (Heb. 4:15). In an amazing manner God showed himself faithful in promise. Great is thy faithfulness! God provided a chief shepherd, a peerless leader, from his very self.

A Lawgiver Like Moses

David was important because he made a deep and lasting impression on temple worship. The Chronicler (the author of 1, 2 Chronicles, Nehemiah, and traditionally Ezra), presented David alongside Moses as a lawgiver for Israel because of David's importance as a leader in worship. Through David's initiative the ark of the covenant came to Jerusalem. Many times a body of the Lord's people is planted by a governmental or business leader, not a "preacher." When David contemplated bringing up the ark, he had a tent or tabernacle constructed to house it (1 Chr. 15:3–16:1). David was also responsible for Jerusalem being the city of worship. He took Jerusalem from the Jebusites, who had managed to retain it for 300 years (1 Chr. 11:4-9). Because of this, Jerusalem was called the city of David. David also initiated systematic steps to organize the music employed at the place of worship (1 Chr. 16:46). The music included both songs and instruments. David encouraged the composing and collecting of psalms and probably wrote a number of the Psalms himself (2 Chr. 29:30). And because of his musical interests, a number of Psalms were dedicated to him. (The superscription translated a Psalm of David, in the Hebrew *le dhawidh,* literally means "to David.")

The laws for priests and sacrifices came through Moses. The laws for the temple music came through David. The Chronicler explicitly sets forth the parallels of David and Moses. These statements reflect the Chronicler's obvious interest in Judah, Jerusalem, and the kings of David. To him David is a new Moses in the sense that he stands with the original lawgiver and adds laws on temple worship which God has decreed. In an interesting passage the juxtaposition of these two lawgivers is obvious. It speaks of the commandment of Moses (2 Chr. 8:13) and the ordinance of David (8:14). These terms are often synonymous in the Old

Testament (Deut. 8:11). Later in this passage David is said to have "commanded" (2 Chr. 8:15; cf. Neh. 12:44-47). David's ordinances for worship were not simply at his own initiative. "The commandment was from the LORD through his prophets" (2 Chr. 29:25).

David was a great man. He was a leader, a shepherd of God's people. He walked with God. He called the people to such a walk. He led the people in worship of God. We need such leadership in the community of believers today. The promise of Yahweh to David interjected eternal hope into the breasts of God's people.

> Afterward the Israelites shall return and seek the LORD their God, and David their king; they shall come in awe to the LORD and to his goodness in the latter days (Hos. 3:5).

Questions for Discussion

1. How did David's early years help qualify him to be king?

2. Why did many thought leaders in Israel reject kingship?

3. Why did God decide to replace Saul so early in his reign?

4. Set forth some of David's political and religious contributions to Israel.

5. Explain the two parts of the Davidic covenant.

6. Why was David, not Solomon, a "man after God's own heart"?

7. The main problem with the Davidic Covenant is the unfaithfulness of the Davidic kings. Can anything be done about this flaw?

8. Can humans always anticipate the manner in which God will execute his covenant, for example, by taking away ten tribes?

9. In view of the promise of an everlasting kingdom explain the end of the Davidic dynasty in the 500s B. C.

10. What seems to be the most crucial aspect of keeping the commandments of God?

11. Why was David paired with Moses as a lawgiver?

12. Were David's rules for worship his own or God's?

11
Praise in the Psalms

We have now examined the major themes in the Old Testament. In the last three chapters of *He Loves Forever* we will notice how some of these themes play out in three major blocks of Old Testament materials: psalms, wisdom, and prophets. We now take up the Psalms.

> Praise the LORD! Praise God in his sanctuary; praise him in his mighty firmament! Praise him for his mighty deeds; praise him according to his surpassing greatness! Let everything that breathes praise the LORD! Praise the LORD! (Ps. 150:1-2,6).

The psalmist of Psalm 150 clearly perceived Yahweh as faithful, loving, and concerned for his people and therefore worthy of praise. For that reason he began every comment with the word "praise." People who intimately walked with God found him continually in their thoughts and on their lips. These thoughts were often written and recorded for future generations. The psalmists reflected on most aspects of private and public existence. However, they concentrated on Yahweh and his way with people. Yahweh came to the rescue in times of trouble. He acted mightily to fashion Israel into a

145

great nation. He forgave and healed. In all his ways, Yahweh was worthy of praise!

Israel's book of worship, the Psalms, reveals the personal struggles and thoughts of the people of God. Later generations preserved, memorized, and relished those psalms which were especially meaningful. The Psalms came from more than five hundred years of Israel's history. They impart to us the heart of Israel's faith. In fact, if all the other documents in the Old Testament were lost, the faith of Israel could be recovered from the Psalms. The songs and hymns of a people often tell much about their thinking and concerns.

A few years ago I knew a song leader who always selected hymns about heaven, Jordan, and Canaan land — mostly old gospel songs. I thought he just preferred those old songs for their rhythm and sentimental value. Then one Sunday night when the preacher was gone, the elders asked this song leader to preach. I immediately noticed that all his remarks were about heaven and getting ready to go there. I began to realize that people sing more about what they are or what they hope to be than they realize. The psalms of Israel tell us who these people were — their failures, their hopes, their joys, their sorrows. But chiefly they tell us of a daily walk with a God who participates moment to moment in the life of each of his children. He did so in the past, he now participates, and he will continue to do so in the future.

How the Psalms Came to Be

The people of God knew of Yahweh down through the centuries not only through his mighty deeds, but also in the retelling of those deeds. Faith was created in Israel by the words of God which revealed what his deeds meant. God creates through words and deeds. In fact, his words result in deeds. "And God said, 'Let the earth bring forth living creatures'" (Gen. 1:24). God created a community of faith through his words and actions. As Yahweh's people sang the psalms, they grew in faith.

The psalms of Israel reflect Yahweh's central concerns for his people and the people's response. They don't give us too many details like dates, places and developments. But they are rich in concepts such as the manner in which the Israelites looked at their world, their reactions to what God had done and was doing in their midst, and their various needs. The songs are basically temple songs, but they reflect private and corporate concerns.

There are basically two purposes of psalms: (1) praise and thanksgiving and (2) laments and petitions. Examining them further, we find six types: (1) psalms of lament (Ps. 13), a majority of the psalms—about 60—are laments; (2) psalms of praise (Ps. 33); (3) temple psalms (Ps. 66); (4) royal psalms about kings (Ps. 45); (5) psalms honoring Yahweh's kingship or enthronement (Ps. 47); and (6) wisdom or instruction psalms (Ps. 1).

It is obvious that the Israelites expressed concern for all phases of their existence through the Psalms. In particular, they brought their personal and national problems to the attention of Yahweh. They also praised God for the times when he answered their complaints. And they expressed hope for the future because they fully expected he would come through again and again. This reminds today's believer of Peter's affirmation, "Cast all your anxiety on him, because he cares for you" (1 Pet. 5:7).

The Face of the Psalms

David, the great king, encouraged the collection of psalms for use in temple worship. Probably some of the psalms even preceded David who started to reign about 1000 B.C. Some of the psalm materials may well have circulated orally for generations before they were written down. Some scholars argue that oral poetry precedes prose. For example, the poems of Homer made up the earliest literature of Greece. They were recited orally long before they were written down. Genesis contains a number of poetic fragments which likely had ancient origins (Gen. 14:19-20; see also Exod. 15:21).

About the time of David's death, priests charged with oversight of the music in the temple collected old psalms, psalms by David, Asaph, Heman and others. A few more were added over the next 150 years, and by Hezekiah's time (about 700 B.C.) the collection totaled more than ninety. Some psalms were written in the northern kingdom (e.g., Ps. 77, 80 and 81) and probably added to the collection at the time of the exile. When the people returned to Palestine in 520 B.C., they tried to reconstitute the faith of old, including temple music (Neh. 12:27-30). The various collections of the psalms were completed in the fifth and fourth centuries B.C.

As the collection of the Psalms came to a close they were divided into five books, possibly on analogy with the five books of the law of Moses. Also beginnings and endings for the books, and perhaps in some cases superscriptions for individual Psalms, were added. The five books are: (1) 1–41, (2) 42–72, (3) 73–89, (4) 90–106, and (5) 107–150. We find a doxology or expression of praise at the end of each book. Psalm 150 may be a doxology to the whole book of Psalms. The beginning of each book contains psalms of lament, but toward the end there are hymns of praise. And there are evidences of smaller collections within the five larger books. At the end of Book II, we read these remarks, "The prayers of David, the son of Jesse, are ended" (Ps. 72:20). All the Psalms of Asaph are found in Book II (73–89), except Psalm 50. Scholars call Psalms 95–100 "enthronement Psalms." Psalms 120–134 include the superscription "A Song of Ascents." These psalms may have been used by the people as they left their homes and traveled to Jerusalem for religious festivals.

Psalms 113–118, which begin and end with "Hallelujah" or "Praise the Lord," are called Hallel Psalms. They probably were sung at the three great feasts. Psalms 146–150 begin and end with "Hallelujah."

The psalms give us a rich, varied collection of the experience of God's people as they attempt to worship and serve him. Therefore, we should be able to discover in Psalms comments which reflect on our situation. When I read for awhile in Psalms, I can always find words to match any mood I am in.

The Psalms represent seven or eight hundred years of walking with God. They came from various times and places. We can therefore readily account for their richness. A key to the whole collection was the praise of Yahweh. "Praise the Lord! O give thanks to the Lord, for he is good; for his steadfast love endures forever!" (Ps. 106:1).

Israel's Identity

The Psalms express the centers of reality from an Old Testament perspective. In them we find a profound declaration of Israel's self-understanding. The identity of Israel was clearly located in its relationship with Yahweh, and the role of each individual in the community of Yahweh's people. That relationship had a past, present and future. Some people of our time locate their identity in the past, such as the Daughters of the American Revolution or religious people who think all the actions of God are long past. Some persons find their identity in the present, like the hippie movement or the proponents of the Social Gospel at the turn of the century. Finally, some obtain their identity from the future, such as the Marxists who believe that because of continuing revolutions Communism will ultimately rule the world, and those Christians who have rejected the present and live in anticipation of the eminent return of Jesus Christ.

Israel took her identity from a God who formed and nurtured a community in the past, a community which lives upon God's good gifts in the present, but which anticipates his continuing actions in the future. They knew who they were because of the community in which they found themselves and the God to whom they belonged. Furthermore, their community and their God was not obstructed in any direction past or present.

Many persons today suffer identity crises. They literally don't know who they are. I once talked with a man who was going through a mental upheaval. He spent some time in a psychiatric hospital. His problem was an identity crisis. As a successful executive of an electronics firm he had all the signs of having it made, but his world had grown hollow. He then lived in another region from the one in which he grew up. This man no longer identified with his home region, and he was schizophrenic about the one where he now lived, because he was not readily accepted there. He didn't belong to any groups, he didn't readily identify with his company, and he was not sure he believed in God. His identity was his work. He had cut himself loose from the past. He had no particular reason to anticipate the future since he had accomplished what he had set out to do with his life. When he realized he had no ties with anything, that he had arrived and that arriving had no meaning of its own, he ended up with a hollow feeling in the pit of his stomach. All was meaningless.

Despite the hope that a person's inner makeup and his present surrounding are adequate ingredients out of which to construct self-identity, people who proceed with this mix ultimately end up in the depths of despair. The grandeur and significance of life in Israel came from the fact that people achieved identity through a community and through a God who had worked in the past, was at work in the present, and had exciting and challenging plans for the future.

From Out of the Past

Israel had roots. The people shared an identity with their parents, grandparents, great-grandparents, aunts, uncles, cousins, and other people from many generations before. The nation had an explicit, personal history. But it was not a do-it-yourself human kind of history. God himself acted in Israel's history. Israel's history was rooted in ultimate reality because it was launched by Yahweh, maker of heaven and earth.

A number of psalms made it explicit that people worshiping Yahweh do so because of the past mighty acts of Yahweh. Psalm 105 praises God for "his deeds among the peoples," and "all his wonderful works" (vv. 1,2). The psalmist mentions the covenant with Abraham, the plagues in Egypt, the exodus, the guidance in the wilderness, the gift of the land, and the laws. God did these "wonderful works" (v. 5) for his people, not just so he could show his muscle. "So he brought his people out with joy, his chosen ones with singing. He gave them the lands of the nations" (vv. 43-44). The joy of Yahweh's people came from God, the one at the heart of reality, the one who supplied to everything its existence, the God of the universe who acted mightily on their behalf and in their very midst. He had given their forefathers identity. To determine who they were, they only needed to remind themselves of how they originated. "Remember the wonderful works he has done, his miracles, and the judgments he uttered, O offspring of his servant Abraham" (vv. 5-6).

Psalm 136 praises the steadfast love of God as shown in his work in creation, the parting of the Red Sea, leading the people in the wilderness, victory over the inhabitants of Palestine, and the gift of the land. All these past acts generated present identity because the same God supplies day-to-day needs to people in the community of faith. "It is he who remembered us in our low estate, for his steadfast love endures forever" (Ps. 136:23). The people of Israel knew who they were and that they were being well cared for because of the one who did many mighty works in their past.

Several psalms also vividly depict God's mighty acts. Psalm 114 celebrates the crossing of the Red Sea and Jordan. "The sea looked and fled; Jordan turned back. The mountains skipped like rams, the hills like lambs" (vv. 3-4). Psalm 135 focused on the conquest, Psalm 8 on creation, Psalm 119 on the law, and Psalm 89 on the promise to David. All these were actions of a God whose existence reached back to eternity. "Before the mountains were brought forth, or ever you had formed the earth and the world, from everlasting to everlasting you are God" (Ps. 90:2).

We are often surprised to read laments, such as Psalms 13 and 35. Despite the fact that the rug seems to have been pulled out from under the psalmist, he doesn't despair. For him, disaster does not result in meaninglessness. He is confident that the God who reversed the headlines in the past will step in and turn present calamities upside down.

The people of Israel also found their identity because of their place in the community of God's people, and not just because of God's mighty works. "Know that the LORD is God. It is he that made us, and we are his; we are his people, and the sheep of his pasture" (Ps. 100:3). Each individual was a member of a flock, a community of people who knew who they were. And because they knew who they were, each individual also knew he belonged in God's flock. When great things happened, each Israelite had a community of people to whom to tell his story. "I have told the glad news of deliverance in the great congregation" (Ps. 40:9). The community's long roots reached into the past. The roots of Israel's history could be summed up in a short poetical statement. Its past was a corporate past. It consisted of Israel's people and their God. Their identity was founded on a rock which cannot be shaken: "O LORD, my rock and my redeemer" (Ps. 19:14).

Israel's God had established the nation's roots in the midst of his congregation of people.

The Ever Present God

Because God acted in Israel's past, the people believed that he was ever present, acting also in the life of each passing generation. The psalmist looked at the past, the future, and the present of each life and saw God in every moment. "You hem me in, behind and before, and lay your hand upon me" (Ps. 139:5). Psalm 18 says whenever God's faithful ones call, he responds. "I call upon the LORD, who is worthy to be praised, so I shall be saved from my enemies" (v. 3). The psalmist also describes the awesome theophany (God's appearance) as Yahweh arrives to assist his servants. "He reached from on high, he took me; he drew me out of mighty waters" (v. 16). Because of God's tremendous assistance, the psalmist's day is a success. "By you I can crush a troop, and by my God I can leap over a wall" (v. 29). Because Israel's roots sank deep in the past, the present had certainty and meaning. No moment of their life was at loose ends, there was no deadening lull after years of strenuous effort, and there was no agonizing over whether anything mattered. The significance of the present lay with the powerful witness from the past.

The people of Yahweh live under the constant watch of Yahweh. "I lie down and sleep; I wake again, for the LORD sustains me" (Ps. 3:5). The message of Psalm 23 has a long-merited significance because this well-known psalm affirms that God cares for his people now as a shepherd cares for his sheep. "He leads me beside still waters; he restores my soul" (Ps. 23:2-3). The present is not vacuous because God walks with his people and they are walking with him. The Lord's people are his sheep. They are a part of a flock. They have their identity from the shepherd and the flock. "For he is our God, and we are the people of his pasture, and the sheep of his hand" (Ps. 95:7). He guides them over the rough spots of life and sustains them. His existence in their present moments is real because he forgives and makes a new life for his people when they stumble. "Create in me a clean heart, O God, and put a new and right spirit within me. . . . Restore to me the joy of your salvation, and sustain in me a willing spirit" (Ps. 51:10,12). The Psalms are sensitive to the present work of God and to his past action. In fact, because of his past action the present is crucial and worthy of concern and discussion.

The Future Is His

Yahweh's people also have assurance that a new dawn will always reveal its telltale streaks of red above the horizon. God's people are firmly anchored to the past, but they are also being winched in from the future. They know where they have been and where they are going. They have no fear of drifting off course and gouging a hole by running on rocks. They know who they are and where they are headed. "But I trust in you, O LORD; I say, 'You are my God.' My times are in your hand; deliver me from the hand of my enemies and persecutors" (Ps. 31:14-15)!

The charge to wait for the Lord tells us that the future is the future of Yahweh. Sometimes the present moment seems untidy. It may be the result of a crisis which has occurred resulting in great stress. Sometimes our detractors seem to have the upper hand. But Yahweh's people never despair even though they suffer many anxious moments (Ps. 44). After all, their identity is not simply the identity of the present moment. If this were the case, as with many today, they would face one crisis and one defeat after another. Each day they would have to ask themselves again who they really are. But Yahweh's people feel a tug from the future. They see the steel cable stretched to the horizon. They wait for the Lord and fully anticipate that he will steer them safely into his desired harbor. "Be strong, and let your heart take courage, all you who wait for the LORD" (Ps. 31:24).

The future is assured because Yahweh himself is everlasting. "From everlasting to everlasting you are God" (Ps. 90:2). Because of his grand works in the past, his people can be sure of their future, "that you may tell the next generation that this is God, our God forever and ever. . . . our guide forever" (Ps. 48:13-14). God has signed his name on the dotted line and committed even the future. "Forever I will keep my steadfast love for him, and my covenant with him will stand firm. I will establish his line forever, and his throne as long as the heavens endure" (Ps. 89:28-29).

Yahweh gave his people songs. He gave them songs even for the blackest moments. He gave songs in the night. Yahweh loves joy. He loves praise. He loves to hear from his people. He loves to help them in their day of trouble. Yahweh loves psalms. "By day the LORD commands his steadfast love, and at night his song is with me, a prayer to the God of my life" (Ps. 42:8).

Questions for Discussion

1. Why was Yahweh worthy of praise?

2. Why do the important theological concepts of Israel show up in the Psalms?

3. Why are there so many Psalms of lament? Is that a problem?

4. What can be said about the authorship of the Psalms?

5. What is the final shape of the book of Psalms? How did the book come to be this way?

6. Why was Israel's past so important for her self-identity?

7. What was the ground in which the roots of Israel were located?

8. How did belonging to the community of faith supply identity?

9. Did the psalmists believe that God acted in their own time?

10. How did the professed future of Israel help establish its identity?

11. Are past, present, and future each important so as to foster identity?

12. What contributions do musical lyrics make to theological reflection?

12
Wisdom through the Proverbs

*J*ust as the psalm tradition in Israel focuses on David, the wisdom tradition centers on Solomon. Solomon attained international notoriety for his wisdom. The acclaim of wisdom in Israel, among her neighbors and people afar off, suggests that wisdom was universally respected. Unlike the laws thundered at Mt. Sinai for the covenant community, the claims of wisdom relate to all men. In its opening statement, Proverbs declares that wisdom is for all men — not just the men of Israel or Judah. "For learning about wisdom and instruction, for understanding words of insight, for gaining instruction in wise dealing, righteousness, justice, and equity" (Prov. 1:2-3).

The queen of Sheba came from her distant country to visit Solomon because she had heard of his wisdom and administrative skill. Sheba was in the southwest corner of modern Saudia Arabia about 1500 miles from Jerusalem. Her visit shows the international interest in wisdom and that wisdom is universally applicable. The queen was impressed by being around Solomon, seeing his kingdom, and hearing his advice (2 Chr. 9:5-7). According to Kings, the wisdom of Solomon "surpassed the wisdom of all the people of the east, and all the wisdom of Egypt" (1 Kgs. 4:30). His proverbs were multifold. "He composed three thousand proverbs, and his songs numbered a thousand and five" (1 Kgs. 4:32).

Though Solomon was the focus of Israel's wisdom, proverbs and other materials came from various sources. The wisdom tradition in Israel possibly began at the town gate where the elders met, business transactions were completed, and judgments made (Ruth 4:1). By Solomon's time the movement obviously centered in the king's court. According to older customs, wise men surrounded the king in Egypt and elsewhere (Gen. 41:8; Dan. 2:12). Jeremiah assigned wise people a special role along with priests and prophets. "For instruction shall not perish from the priest, nor counsel from the wise, nor the word from the prophet" (Jer. 18:18). There were family or clan wisdom, courtly wisdom, scribal wisdom, nature wisdom, and juridical and practical wisdom. And there was the special wisdom of warriors, sailors, farmers, and soothsayers.

The Shape of Proverbs

Though many proverbs are assigned to Solomon, some come from other authors. Later collections in the book of Proverbs, gathered by wisemen, didn't all come from Solomon. However, there is no reason to deny that Solomon wrote many proverbs.

The first heading in Proverbs is titled, "the proverbs of Solomon son of David, King of Israel" (1:1). A second heading states, "The proverbs of Solomon" (10:1). A third heading asserts that an additional collection was made of Solomon's proverbs in the days of Hezekiah, more than 200 years after Solomon's death (25:1). Two other headings attribute material to non-Israelite sources: "The words of Agur son of Jakeh"

(Prov. 30:1), and "The words of King Lemuel" (Prov. 31:1). There was a willingness to receive wisdom from more than one source and even sources outside Israel.

The form and content of the sayings in Proverbs also differ. Proverbs 1–9 is different from Proverbs 10–22:17. The material in the first nine chapters contains ideas developed in more lengthy passages. The literary structure has continuity for several verses. Much more interest in God is evident, and his name is mentioned more often. The proverbs between chapters 10 and 22:17 are almost all two-line proverbs. The subject matter from one proverb to another may or may not relate to the same topic. The form most often found is antithetical parallelism: "A wise child loves discipline, but a scoffer does not listen to rebuke" (Prov. 13:1). Notice the antithesis between "wise son" and "scoffer," "instruction" and "rebuke." Although this section occasionally refers to God, the theological flavor in these proverbs borders on the minuscule.

Other wisdom materials in the Old Testament are Job, Ecclesiastes, and Song of Songs, as well as various Psalms and sections in prophetic books.

We need also to consider the nature of "wisdom" found in the Old Testament. If you have done much reading in Job or Proverbs, you may have a feel for what wisdom means. If not, you may at first be surprised. To us, wisdom means either technical knowledge, such as the technology of space flight; expert information, such as a tax lawyer knowing how to set up a foundation; or intellectual insight, such as a philosopher mastering the ideas of Immanuel Kant. This wisdom, however, is not the wisdom of the Old Testament. In the Old Testament, wisdom is the art of picking your way through life with a minimum of bumps and bruises. It is practical knowledge about rules governing the world and the relationships between people. People acquire this wisdom through experience, and they accumulate it through generations. The total experience from the perspective of spiritual values is transferred from father to son. Wisdom is the ability to cope and say the right word or do the right deed at the right time.

Where Does Wisdom Come From?

Anyone who reads Deuteronomy and Leviticus, then turns to Proverbs, will notice considerable differences. Deuteronomy and Leviticus consist of laws for a covenant community, for internal and external relations, and for cultic celebration. Proverbs contains rules for life, the right path to travel, the right voice to hear. But despite the differences, both have a common source, God. Law and wisdom belong in the same book because they both come from God. But the manner in which they come from God differs. The people for whom law and wisdom are intended are the same, except that wisdom is for all men, not just the covenant community.

How do the insights of wisdom come from God? The word of God in the law was delivered to Moses directly on Mt. Sinai. The word of Yahweh came through the prophets in pictures, objects, and words, without any effort on the part of the prophets. Wisdom obviously was not a part of the law delivered on the mountain. It didn't arrive as a voice or in a vision from God. How do wise men become wise? They learn what their fathers passed on.

> Listen, children, to a father's instruction, and be attentive, that you may gain insight; for I give you good precepts: do not forsake my teaching. When I was a son with my father, tender, and my mother's favorite, he taught me, and said to me . . . (Prov. 4:1-4).

But how did the fathers learn what they passed on? Most likely the fathers learned by observing the ways of life and the world, and by studying which path creates the least friction. Wisdom results from "heads up," astute sifting of experience. It is not the experience of one person. It is the accumulated, scrutinized experience of many generations.

But if wisdom results from human effort, how can it come from God? Is what comes through human experience and what comes from God the same?

Let's start with a "yes" answer and see what data is available before responding "no." In wisdom literature we read that creation and history reflect the wisdom of God because through wisdom he created that which exists. The word of God in the wisdom materials is related to the mighty acts of God in creation. "The LORD by wisdom founded the earth; by understanding he established the heavens; by his knowledge the deeps broke open, and the clouds drop down the dew" (Prov. 3:19-20).

Proverbs 8:22-31 expands on this theme. Creation itself bears the telltale signs of the ways of God. We discern the ways of God when we observe nature and life. Just as we learn the ways of the artist by studying Picasso's "Guernica," so we can discover the ways of God by studying nature. Therefore, when people sort out the ways of nature through experience, their conclusions come from God because they are God's ways. This is the argument of natural or universal ethics. Universal ethics operate on the premise that all men can know right by studying the ways of nature because God is the author of nature.

The Position of the Scriptures

But the position which assumes that the discovery is totally human is ostensibly not the position of the Scriptures. First, the text says the wisdom of Solomon came neither from his earthly father nor solely from his own powers of observation. It came from God. "God gave Solomon very great wisdom, discernment, and breadth of understanding as vast as the sand on the seashore" (1 Kgs. 4:29).

How did God give Solomon wisdom? Was it through oracles or a direct delivery of his word, the manner in which he spoke to the prophets? The answer apparently is no. Yahweh said to Solomon, "Indeed I give you a wise and discerning mind; no one like you shall arise after you" (1 Kgs. 3:12). God gave Solomon a mind for wisdom, and he acquired specific insight through his own observation and struggle. But perhaps the conclusions were not left purely to the powers of the mind. Proverbs 2 attributes the acquiring of wisdom, first of all, to strenuous human effort. A person must listen to the words of wisdom, then struggle and cry out for insight (2:3). He must work hard and diligently seek wisdom, just as he would put in long, hard hours searching for treasure (2:4). After all this effort, then "you will understand the fear of the LORD and find the knowledge of God." (Prov. 2:5).

This may be like a person who struggles over the nature of light for several months, then finally comes up with a brilliant answer in a flash. Similarly, a person struggles through astute observations and finally attains wisdom, but it is God who supplies the flash. We conclude that wisdom comes from God because: (1) the observer examines nature and life, in which the ways of God are found; (2) he persistently weighs and sifts through his experiences with a mind given by God; and (3) he ultimately arrives at a conclusion after his struggle. But God provides the insight at the end of the struggle. In this manner wisdom is, in fact, from God. The proverbs are his words. But the channel through which the word of God arrives differs from the channel through which law and prophecy come.

For whom is wisdom intended? Based on circumstantial evidence in the text, wisdom is for all humans. The covenant community is an appropriate recipient for wisdom since it is from God. The covenant community is also subject to the laws of God delivered at Mt. Sinai. But the law given at Sinai was for Israel alone, not the nations, and only occasionally did the other nations receive instructions from God through the prophets. But the nations also can know rules for right living by a close look at nature's ethical laws.

Yahweh is the God of the nations. He is concerned with all men. God transplanted people other than Israel (Amos 9:7). Amos and other prophets condemned the nations because they should have known better by observations of right and wrong from life and nature. "So they are without excuse" (Rom. 1:20). In the Old Testament, the ways of Yahweh are most obvious in the commands Moses brought down from the mountain and in the oracles of the prophet who declares, "Thus says the word of the Lord." Nevertheless, traces of the ways of God are visible in life and nature, and God provides insight to those who seek long and hard. The ways of God are available to all humans, and all are accountable.

The Message of Wisdom

The message of wisdom is directed to all Israelites and persons everywhere. The sons of Israel share with all men the knowledge that Yahweh is maker of heaven and earth and that all people bear his image. Through the wisdom tradition, the Old Testament recognizes the common situation of all men in the world and their common concerns and solutions. In many periods of Israel's history, the law and words from the prophets overshadowed wisdom. But wisdom remains, and occasionally it surfaces when times are appropriate. These are times when human reflection and observation are prized and people search for universal rights and wrongs, not just beliefs of a particular religious tradition.

The message of wisdom is multifaceted, but the basic convictions are that (1) the world is orderly because of Yahweh's "wisdom" at work in creation; (2) the wise people who tune into the orderly features of creation give advice which will improve the quality and length of life; (3) God

made the universe so that virtue is rewarded and vice punished; and (4) people must fear the Lord, not just know the
ways of God. One must also fear the Lord to have the com-
pulsion and humility to actually live wisely.

1. The world is orderly. The orderliness of creation is perhaps most clearly expressed in Ecclesiastes. "For everything
there is a season, and a time for every matter under heaven:
a time to be born, and a time to die" (Eccl. 3:1). Everything
has a time, but it is repeated. Nothing changes. The universe
is like an army marching in place. There is movement, but the
same motion is repeated over and over. There is "a time to
plant, and a time to pluck up what is planted" (3:2). Planting
changes to harvesting, but planting and harvesting continue
like clockwork. The world is orderly because whatever happens is repeated at predictable intervals. "That which is,
already has been; that which is to be, already is; and God
seeks out what has gone by" (3:15). If anything in the universe drops out of line, God hustles it back in place.

The fact that wisdom was with God when he created the
earth also expresses confidence in the orderliness of creation.

> When he established the heavens, I was there, when he drew a cir-
> cle on the face of the deep, when he made firm the skies above, when
> he established the fountains of the deep, when he assigned to the sea
> its limit, so that the waters might not transgress his command, when
> he marked out the foundations of the earth, then I was beside him
> (Prov. 8:27-30).

God's faithfulness is as obvious in creation as it is in his
promises and their fulfillment. God loves the created order
forever. Therefore, he loves wisdom forever because it seeks
order in creation.

2. Wisdom discovers the quality of life. The purpose of wisdom is to give "instruction in wise dealing, righteousness, justice, and equity; to teach shrewdness to the simple, knowledge and prudence to the young" (Prov. 1:3-4). The person

who follows wisdom will have well-being, pleasantness, and long life.

> Happy are those who find wisdom, and those who get understanding, for her income is better than silver, and her revenue better than gold. She is more precious than jewels, and nothing you desire can compare with her. Long life is in her right hand; in her left hand are riches and honor. Her ways are ways of pleasantness, and all her paths are peace. She is a tree of life to those who lay hold of her; those who hold her fast are called happy (Prov. 3:13-18).

Even the author of Ecclesiastes, who sometimes thinks that in the end the wise man is no better off than the fool, nevertheless, believes that wisdom adds to the quality of life, just as money does.

> Wisdom is as good as an inheritance, an advantage to those who see the sun. For the protection of wisdom is like the protection of money, and the advantage of knowledge is that wisdom gives life to the one who possesses it (Eccl. 7:11-12).

God created the universe using wisdom. The person therefore who discovers the signs of wisdom in the world and lives accordingly will come out on top because he is living life according to God's rules. Just as a locomotive can pull a heavier load and last longer by running on tracks because it was built to run on tracks, a life which proceeds according to the rules of the universe will be longer and have well-being.

3. Virtue is rewarded and vice punished. If the world is orderly and God is good, then the universe must be designed so that people get ahead by doing right and they are set back by doing wrong. Wisdom talks little about punishment and reward after death because virtue is rewarded and wickedness is punished in this life. These rewards and punishments do not require special acts of God. Rewards and punishments result naturally from the world. For example, work has its rewards, but laziness has its punishment (Prov. 10:4). People who do right have nothing to worry about, but wrongdoers live in fear (Prov. 10:9).

A person who defies the demands of the marriage relationship will suffer the consequences. God may not throw a thunderbolt out of heaven and paralyze him for two weeks or strike him dead, but the world is built so that the jealousy of a man toward his wife's lover will bring about punishment (Prov. 6:27-35).

Job and Ecclesiastes, however, suggest that too simple an explanation of rewards and punishment tends to be disillusioning. Job was as virtuous as any, but he suffered the loss of flocks, herds, and family. The writer of Ecclesiastes says, "In my vain life I have seen everything; there are righteous people who perish in their righteousness, and there are wicked people who prolong their life in their evildoing" (Eccl. 7:15).

However, neither of these books denies that, for the most part, virtue is rewarded and evil punished. They are concerned with the exceptions. How are these explained? Ecclesiastes may not offer an answer, except that there is an element of the unpredictable from where humans stand, but not from God's perspective. Since people cannot look over the shoulder of God to see what he is up to, they must accept their status and enjoy whatever comes their way in life. Job, however, suggests that life is more complex than many people think. God's decisions, not just the rules built into the earth, determine the course of a person's life. The exceptions are explained by God's actions in his total universe to bring about his ways.

It would seem, therefore, that taking existence as a whole, rewards and punishments flow naturally in the universe. But from the human perspective various exceptions are observed. These may ultimately be explained, but to do so one has to sit in on the heavenly council. We do not have enough facts to know why everything happens as it does. "Hollywood life styles" seem to create more anguish, dysfunction and shorter life spans than the average population. Going by this, doing right wins out and wickedness loses. But man doesn't understand in every case just how this happens, and he doesn't know all the interests and workings of God.

4. The fear of the Lord. It's not enough just to know. Knowledge may simply make a person a dilettante, someone who professes a love of wisdom, art, and ethics, but who shows by the way he lives that he really doesn't care. According to the wisdom tradition, it does a person no good to gain all the insights of wisdom if she is not humble or doesn't feel compelled to do what she knows is right. Solomon was a great king because of his wisdom, but he met disaster because he did not fear the Lord. His pride and wrong desires canceled his great wisdom (1 Kgs. 11:9-10). Therefore, wisdom has no efficacy unless it is founded upon fear. "The fear of the LORD is the beginning of knowledge; fools despise wisdom and instruction" (Prov. 1:7). People who gain from wisdom are people who fear the Lord enough to find out his intentions for man in the world, then set out to live accordingly.

The Lord loves wisdom forever. Through it he has created the heavens and the earth. He is committed to a relationship with his creation forever. He loves people who seek out his ways through the created order. They are usually the ones who live long, productive, rewarding lives.

Questions for Discussion

1. How did the revelation on Sinai differ from wisdom viewed as revelation?

2. Was the wisdom tradition limited to Israel?

3. In what sort of places in Israel did wisdom flourish?

4. What is known about the authorship of Proverbs?

5. What is the nature of wisdom in the wisdom tradition?

6. How does Proverbs 1–9 differ from 10–22:17?

7. How did wisdom and insight come about? In what sense was it from God?

8. How is wisdom grounded in the mighty acts of God?

9. Why is it that in observing the outcomes of human actions, persons discover the ways of God?

10. What are the basic points of view underlying wisdom?

11. Does vice always get punished and virtue rewarded?

12. Why is fear of the Lord important if wisdom is to be appropriated?

13
Hope of the Prophets

The Old Testament ends as it begins by affirming the steadfast love of the Lord. But from the human aspect, it doesn't look as good as it did in the beginning. Through the 1,500 years since the promise of Yahweh to Abraham, humans continually sinned. They made up their own rules for life and lived by them rather than following the loving laws of God. "The Lord saw that the wickedness of humankind was great in the earth, and that every inclination of the thoughts of their hearts was only evil continually" (Gen. 6:5). "All we like sheep have gone astray; we have all turned to our own way, and the Lord has laid on him the iniquity of us all" (Isa. 53:6). Despite humanity's waywardness, however, God remained faithful in his relentless love. The Old Testament ends on a positive note by telling us that the time is coming when God will break into history in a new and amazing way and dwell with humans so that they will continually walk in loving obedience. Yahweh never gives up. He always comes up with astoundingly new ways of wooing humans to himself.

I am about to do a new thing (Isa. 43:19).

Some stories aren't complete. They promise future action which remains unfulfilled. The story line of the Old Testament includes promises which go unfulfilled, and it talks of new ages which never arrive. The Old Testament points beyond itself. It heralds an age or a person which or who has not yet appeared. The Jews still look for a messianic age or a messiah. In contrast, the early Christians declared that all the unfulfilled hopes came to fruition in an amazing manner in Jesus of Nazareth. The good news of Jesus Christ tells us that all those items left dangling at the close of the Old Testament were gathered and tied together in his ministry, his death, his resurrection, his kingdom, and his future appearance.

Messengers of Hope

In particular, the prophets of Israel offer hope for the future. The prophets spent much time demanding current obedience and justice. They frequently commented on what would soon come to pass if God's people did not repent and change their ways. But sometimes they burst forth in unrestrained optimism over future divine actions.

> So the ransomed of the LORD shall return, and come to Zion with singing; everlasting joy shall be upon their heads; they shall obtain joy and gladness, and sorrow and sighing shall flee away (Isa. 51:11).

The prophetic movement actually began in the days of Samuel, or the 1100s B.C. Bands of prophets commenced to appear at this time (1 Sam. 19:20). Later, in the period of the kings, the prophets rose to prominence. They served as the conscience of the nation. They counterbalanced the power of the kings and princes. Their function was like the media persons of today, except that prophets professed to bring a word from the Lord.

Nathan, Elijah, and Elisha, the first great prophets, encouraged the kings to be God's men. When the kings violated the law of God, Nathan, Elijah, and Elisha responded with words of condemnation. Few direct statements from these prophets have been preserved. It was not until the eighth century B.C. that oracles of prophets were written on scrolls. The written utterances of these prophets are divided into major and minor, but this has nothing to do with their importance. It refers to the length of their work. The four major prophets (Isaiah, Jeremiah, Ezekiel, and Daniel) are followed by twelve minor prophets. One way of grouping which helps put each prophet in perspective is by the century in which he worked. The fact that we know the time of the prophets is more important than we realize. It tells us that God entered into the actual life of men in the Old Testament. There is no way of dating the work of the gods in the Hindu scriptures. Their actions seldom interfaced with real human history. But Yahweh involves himself in the life and history of his people. The earliest prophets who wrote and whose writings are preserved, lived in the eighth century B.C.

Here are the prophets and their century:

Eighth: Amos, Hosea, Isaiah, Micah, Jonah (?)

Seventh: Jeremiah, Zephaniah, Nahum

Sixth: Habakkuk, Ezekiel, Obadiah, Haggai, Zechariah

Fifth: Daniel, Malachi, Joel (?)

The later prophets more often searched the distant horizon for signs of extraordinary divine activity.

The future hopes and promises at the close of the Old Testament may be divided into five parts. The details vary from prophet to prophet and some affirmations occur more frequently than others. In order of frequency, they are (1) new actions of Yahweh, (2) a new age, (3) a new reign, (4) a new ruler, and (5) a new relationship.

New Actions of Yahweh

Israel believed that Yahweh would break into history in amazingly new ways in the future because he had acted powerfully in the past. Earlier when Israel cried out to God, he heard the cry and responded lovingly. Israel believed that the steadfast love of the Lord never ceased, so the people saw no reason to conclude that the deeds of God were all past. He could repeat his actions. He could create anew, open new paths through the sea, be with his people in a new wilderness, and give his people new victories. These convictions had important ramifications for all persons who later walked with God. They declare he always works in new and creative ways, loving and caring for his people. "But if God so clothes the grass of the field, which is alive today and tomorrow is thrown into the oven, will he not much more clothe you — you of little faith?" (Matt. 6:30).

The most traumatic experience of the people of Israel in Old Testament times was the destruction of Jerusalem in 587 B.C. by the Babylonian army. In the word of the Lord which came to Jeremiah, the destruction was so catastrophic that it constituted a reversal of creation (Jer. 4:23-26). But after the catastrophe, Yahweh started over again. He created plants, animals, and people.

> The days are surely coming, says the Lord, when I will sow the house of Israel and the house of Judah with the seed of humans and the seed of animals. And just as I have watched over them to pluck up and break down, to overthrow, destroy, and bring evil, so I will watch over them to build and to plant, says the Lord (Jer. 31:27-28).

Once in a while our world falls to pieces. It may be a personal tragedy like the death of a husband, or a national tragedy like the war in Viet Nam. But Yahweh recreates his world. He brings beauty from ashes. In Ezekiel's valley of dry bones, God laid sinews, flesh, and skin on the decaying bits of calcium, and they amazingly came to life (Ezek. 37:1-6).

God's work is not over. He is always doing new things. "Do not remember the former things, or consider the things of old. I am about to do a new thing; now it springs forth, do you not perceive it?" (Isa. 43:18-19). Isaiah's convictions about the continuing work of God were so strong that he declared Yahweh would "create new heavens and a new earth" (Isa. 65:17).

The prophets also believed God would favor them with new exoduses. Isaiah looked past the destruction of Jerusalem to a new exodus (Isa. 43:16-19). Deuteronomy predicted that God would reverse his action if his people were unfaithful. "The LORD will bring you back in ships to Egypt" (Deut. 28:68). With great expectation, Jeremiah envisioned a new exodus for the people of God beyond their bondage (Jer. 23:7-8).

The people of God continue to be enslaved by debts, family problems, and even alcoholism. They bring their problems on themselves just as Israel did through its sin. But if God's people will cry out to him and repent of their evil works, he will hear them and open up new paths through the sea.

The prophets also anticipated a new wilderness where God would love his people freely and where the gulfs between God and man, man and man, and man and animal would be bridged (Hos. 2:14-15). Isaiah depicted a wilderness and spoke of a highway through it (Isa. 35:5-8). The Hebrews writer said Jesus provided a new day in the wilderness, and Christians committed to him would rest from their labors (Heb. 4:1-10).

When Israel gloriously took the land with great victories, it signaled future expectation that God's enemies are always doomed. God gave great victories to his people in the past, and he will give them victories again (Zech. 14:4-5). "The LORD, your God, is in your midst, a warrior who gives victory" (Zeph. 3:17). People today have been frightened "out of their wits" by movies about Armageddon and the destruction of the "late, great planet earth." Of course, unbelievers should obviously tremble. But people who know of the victories of "the Lion of the tribe of Judah," the son of Yahweh, are confident, not fearful. He has conquered (Rev. 5:5). No enemy is too great for our God. He loves to give new victories. In fact, because of the victory already won by Jesus, the awesome battle shaping up with Gog and Magog is no contest. They are dispatched by God in one fell swoop (Rev. 20:9). Great are the victories of God!

A New Age

The prophets anticipated a new day when God's presence will be more obvious than in the past. This new era will include the dissemination of the law of Yahweh among all the peoples of the earth, the worship of nation with nation, the flowering of peace, and a universal language.

Both Isaiah and Micah spoke of a new age when numerous persons would actually desire to hear the laws of the Lord. In turn they would carry them back to their friends. The loving ways of Yahweh would then prevail upon the earth. His good gifts would benefit all the inhabitants of the earth. A new love and peace would be obvious everywhere (Isa. 2:2-4; Micah 4:1-4).

> Many peoples shall come and say, "Come, let us go up to the mountain of the LORD, to the house of the God of Jacob; that he may teach us his ways and that we may walk in his paths." For out of Zion shall go forth instruction, and the word of the LORD from Jerusalem (Isaiah 2:3).

Isaiah even envisioned major powers worshiping Yahweh together and being at peace with one another (Isa. 19:23; cf. Mic. 7:11-17).

In Zephaniah's beautiful vision of all the nations coming together, some were destroyed, but some were also preserved in order to create a new serving people. Yahweh is still looking for people through whom he will bless the nations. The new people he will call can disseminate their message far and wide because they will speak one language. "At that time I will change the speech of the peoples to a pure speech, that all of them may call on the name of the LORD and serve him with one accord" (Zeph. 3:9-10). The new breakthrough of Yahweh is also called the "day of the Lord" (Joel 1:15; Mal. 4:1-5).

This new age had still not arrived as the Old Testament ended. But the people who ate and slept and walked with Jesus believed the prophets had the age of his ministry and church in mind. People from the far corners of the earth heard the good news of the resurrection of Jesus on a visit to Jerusalem (Acts 2). Because of him, people from all the nations worshiped together. He brought peace on earth by teaching that his followers should even love their enemies (Matt. 5:43-48; cf. 5:9). And as people from all nations heard the declaration of God's work in Christ, amazingly they each heard the message in their own language. All heard and understood the new message of God (Acts 2:6).

Some of the implications of these prophecies, however, possibly have not yet been fulfilled. Some people insist that none of these promises have come to fruition. They believe the promises have to do with precise developments in a rapture and a thousand-year reign of Christ on earth. They obviously ignore the new day of God which happened in Jesus. On the other hand, people who insist that all prophecy is highly imaginative, overly figurative, and without literal significance may someday be in for a rude awakening. After tracing the promises of God through the Old Testament, it should be obvious that we are often surprised by joy. Yahweh still has work to do in this world. The prophets encourage us always to be open to the future in expectation. Knowing the sort of god Yahweh is, we must take precautions against a hardening of the categories.

Yahweh will be what he will be. We believe the future is his, but what we can be sure of in his future is only a sketchy outline. He will provide the details. We witness the action, wait for the dust to settle, and then piece together how the fulfillment matches the promise. We therefore stand before these prophetic visions in both certainty and uncertainty. We know that the future of the world is in the hands of God and he will do the unexpected. But we can never anticipate God's specific actions, despite popular contemporary preachers who claim inside information and confide that by the Bible they can declare tomorrow's headlines today. It is enough to know that God is at the helm. We may not know what the future brings, but we can know the one who brings the future.

A New Reign and a New Ruler

Some prophets apparently had in mind that in a future day Yahweh would restore the political kingdoms of David and Solomon. Amos anticipated that after destruction Yahweh would restore the fortunes of his people (Amos 9:14). However, the prophet who highlighted the new reign or kingdom was Daniel.

In Daniel, God's people are in exile. They are evicted from the promised land. Rather than praising Yahweh in Jerusalem, they were weeping by the river Chedbar (Ezek. 1:1). Daniel had a grand vision of a succession of mighty empires, more than just an endless rise and fall of civilizations. Each successive fall of an empire set the stage for the break-in of a new rule, the rule of Yahweh himself. "And in the days of those kings the God of heaven will set up a kingdom that shall never be destroyed, nor shall this kingdom be left to another people. It shall crush all these kingdoms and bring them to an end, and it shall stand forever" (Dan. 2:44). Paul declared that Christians are situated in just such a kingdom. "He has rescued us from the power of darkness and transferred us to the kingdom of his beloved Son" (Col. 1:13; cf. 1 Cor. 15:25).

Tied in with the new reign and inseparable from it is a new ruler from the family of David. "A shoot shall come out from the stump of Jesse, and a branch shall grow out of his roots" (Isa. 11:1). Most of these passages speak of a new king from the family of David, a human being like the former ones, but having new qualities of loyalty to Yahweh. But perhaps there are clues that Yahweh will bring forth a succession of new kings and, at some crucial juncture, a descendant of David with unanticipated powers and connections.

In Micah 5:2 the prophet spoke of a ruler born in Bethlehem "whose origin is from of old, from ancient days." We need to remember that David was born in Bethlehem (1 Sam. 17:12). That was 300 years before Micah. Therefore, the scion of David that Micah anticipated had roots reaching back for 300 years. His origin is "from of old" (5:2). He will be a majestic leader of God's people. "And he shall stand and feed his flock in the strength of the LORD, in the majesty of the name of the LORD his God" (Mic. 5:4). Christians understood that, in a special sense, Jesus fulfilled this anticipation.

Isaiah 9 envisions a mighty king descended from David. As John Willis wrote in his *Living Word Commentary* on Isaiah, all the terms of Isaiah 9:6-7 are and may be applied to an earthly king from David. This is true, but we cannot limit the work of God. He may even have in mind here a scion who was his very own Son. Obviously, the early Christians anticipated a human messiah (Mark 10:35-45). They were surprised by joy, however, when the resurrection confirmed that he was God's very Son (Acts 2:36).

Daniel 7 gives the clearest affirmation of a heavenly figure receiving a kingdom. "His dominion is an everlasting

dominion that shall not pass away" (Dan. 7:14). The phrase
"like a son of man" (v. 13, NIV), means that the one to
receive the kingdom was not a man, but like one. He was
either less or more than man. The implication clearly is that
he was more. By the first century the Jews were talking about
a new king (an anointed one, messiah) a new messianic kingdom, and a messianic age. Daniel 7 has such a king and kingdom in mind. For the early Christians, this figure "like a son
of man" was obviously Jesus himself. By his use of the title
"son of man," he shows that he identified with this prediction
and claimed divine origins for himself. For the first-century
believers, even the language of Daniel 7 describes the coming
again of Jesus. "Then they will see 'the Son of Man coming
in clouds' with great power and glory" (Mark 13:26).

The section of Isaiah beginning with chapter 40 frequently speaks of a figure who will appear in Israel's future —
a servant. The servant is the channel through whom God will
bring his blessings to the nations (Isa. 49:6). It is not real
clear who this servant is. Sometimes the servant is Israel (Isa.
49:3). By Isaiah 53:8, if not earlier, the servant turns out to
be an individual who has suffered for Yahweh's own people,
as well as for the nations.

Who is this servant? Is he a prophet, priest, or king, or
simply a common citizen picked for this role? This text makes
no reference to the servant as a kingly or divine figure. But
the text does not **limit** how God will fulfill his word. The
early Christians believed the servant was Jesus, descendant of
David, the anointed king of God's new people, God's very
Son (Acts 8:26-40).

A New Relationship

The prophets anticipated that God himself would provide the remedy for man's sin by giving him a new heart and
a new spirit (Ezek. 36:26). When that happens, man will be

faithful to God, creating a new relationship. "I will put my spirit within you, and make you follow my statutes and be careful to observe my ordinances" (Ezek. 36:27). Jeremiah referred to the new relationship as a new covenant. "I will make a new covenant with the house of Israel and the house of Judah" (Jer. 31:31). In the new relationship God will "put my law within them, and I will write it on their hearts; and I will be their God, and they shall be my people" (Jer. 31:33).

For Paul the new relationship came through the arrival of Jesus. The Holy Spirit also put in an appearance at the same time (Gal. 3:1-5). Ezekiel said that the spirit of God would cause his people to walk in his statutes. Paul said, "If we live by the Spirit, let us also be guided by the Spirit" (Gal. 5:25). He clearly understood the fruit of the Spirit as the fulfilling of the law of God through Christ (Gal. 6:2).

His Loves Endures Forever

The God of the Old Testament has shown himself through all the days and years as a God who loves man, the being made in his image. He is immersed in a continual struggle, working daily with his servants, preparing them as warehouse managers who will dispense his good gifts to the nations.

But as the Old Testament comes to a close, it is not all over. Many statements provide assurances that, over the horizon in some future age, Yahweh will break into history in a new and decisive manner. The New Testament tells us the good news that it actually happened. "Blessed be the God and Father of our Lord Jesus Christ, who has blessed us in Christ with every spiritual blessing in the heavenly places" (Eph. 1:3). In the new day of Jesus Christ, the steadfast love of Yahweh descended upon all creation.

O give thanks to the LORD, for he is good, for his steadfast love endures forever (Ps. 136:1).

Questions for Discussion

1. Does the Old Testament seem complete in itself?

2. What are some of the promises that go unfulfilled?

3. When did the prophetic movement begin and what was its purpose?

4. What is the distinction between major and minor prophets?

5. What are some of the main projections about the future in the prophets?

6. Give some examples in which Yahweh will repeat his mighty works in new and powerful ways?

7. What are characteristics of the new age envisioned by the prophets?

8. Which is more important, to know the future or the one who holds the future?

9. How will a new Davidic ruler play a role in the future?

10. What are the clues that the new Davidic ruler might be the very Son of Yahweh?

11. How will humans in the future be related to Yahweh in a new manner?

12. Is the open-ended Old Testament ever completed? How?

About the Author

Thomas H. Olbricht was born in Thayer, Missouri. He received degrees from Northern Illinois University, the University of Iowa, and Harvard Divinity School. He has served Churches of Christ as a minister in Illinois, Iowa, Massachusetts, and Pennsylvania and as an elder in Abilene, Texas, and Malibu, California. Olbricht has taught at Harding University, The University of Dubuque, The Pennsylvania State University, Abilene Christian University, and Pepperdine University from which he retired in 1996. He has published ten books, written articles in fifty others, and has served as editor of and published in several journals. He and Dorothy, his wife of almost fifty years, live in South Berwick, Maine. They have five children and twelve grandchildren.

College Press Publishing Company, Inc.

Other Books By Thomas Olbricht:
His Love Compels

Related Titles Published by College Press:
Falling in Love with Jesus by Rubel Shelly
Yet Will I Trust Him by John Mark Hicks

*College Press produces Bible Commentaries,
Small Group Studies, Sunday School Materials,
Vacation Bible School Materials, and Christian
Books on a variety of topics.
To See These Products:*

Contact Your Local Bookstore

Or

College Press Publishing Company, Inc.
1-800-289-3300 Toll Free
email *books@collegepress.com*
Visit our web page at
www.collegepress.com